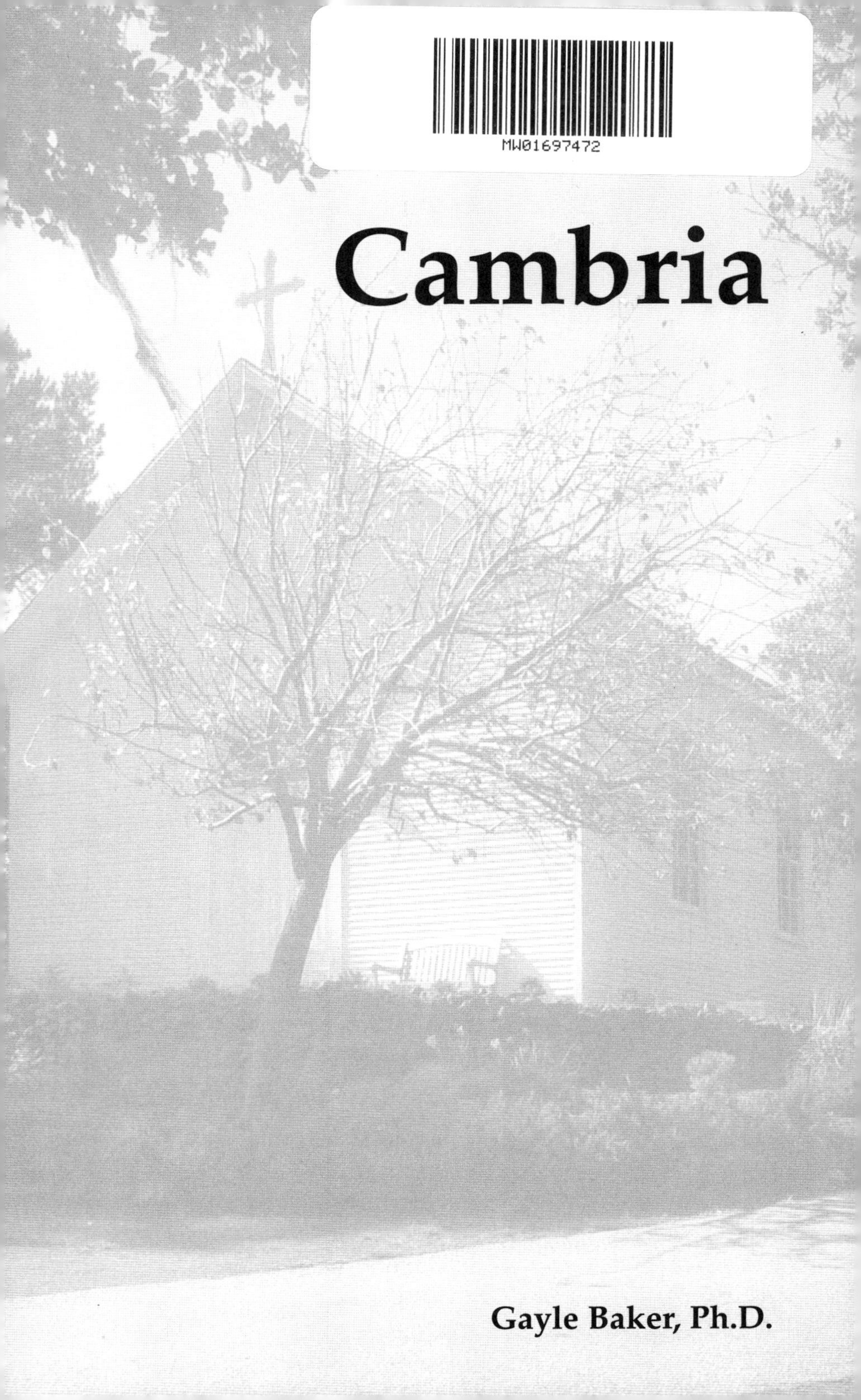

Cambria

Gayle Baker, Ph.D.

Other books by the author:

The Wet Mountain Valley, 1975

Trial and Triumph, 1977

Catalina Island, 2002

Santa Barbara, 2003

Printed in Canada by Hignell Book Printing

Library of Congress Cataloging in Publication Data:

Baker, Gayle
Cambria/Gayle Baker, Ph.D.
1st p. cm. ed.
Includes index.
ISBN 0-9710984-2-5
History of Cambria, California
History of San Luis Obispo County
I. Title

PCN 2003108568

*Cover by **Larry Iwerks,** renowned Santa Barbara watercolorist*

All historical photos are from

The Wilfred Lyons Collection

Lyons Store, next to Soto's Market, 1930s

1911 Parade

Table of Contents

Main road into Cambria, 1895

Bridge Street, 1888

Before Cambria Was Cambria

Nestled among the pines at the junction of the coast road and Santa Rosa Creek, Cambria was blessed with plentiful lumber, a stunning coastline, fertile agricultural land, and hills rich with quicksilver. In this small corner of California's picturesque Central Coast, speculators would buy land, entrepreneurs would build a vibrant supply and service center, miners would come to relax and party after long hours in nearby mines, and dairymen would prosper.

Cambria citizens would be infected by mining fever when promising veins of quicksilver were discovered, mourn a fire that devastated their downtown, and work together to rescue the crew of a tanker torpedoed just off their coast. They would face disappointment when the railroad replaced shipping, and, again, when the highway to Hearst Castle detoured around their town. Instead, they participated in the building of an amazing castle and began to welcome visitors from around the world to San Luis Obispo County.

Today Cambria is a favorite locale in which to enjoy ocean sunsets, watch gifted artists work, wander through the lovely Victorian village, enjoy a great restaurant, and relax at one of its wonderful inns. It took Cambria years of trials and triumphs to acquire its unique place as one of California's most fascinating towns. Its story begins with local tribes, nearby missions, and two enormous land grants.

Local Tribes

Although our recorded history of the tribes in the region does not begin until the explorers and missionaries arrived, there is evidence that there were many tribal settlements in the area that was to become Cambria. It is estimated that as many as 30,000 Native Americans thrived in the San Luis Obispo area in the 1000 years before the Spaniards arrived.

Some experts believe that these tribes were migratory and used Cambria only as a seasonal settlement, while others are convinced that they lived there permanently. Most agree that they feasted on shellfish and seafood on the coast, in addition to traveling inland to hunt and gather seeds. A variety of their artistically crafted implements have been discovered, including obsidian spears and arrowheads; basalt, sandstone, and granite mortars and pestles; soapstone kettles; and stone hammers. Tribesmen were skilled basket and net makers and fashioned jewelry from crab claws, abalone shells, and the teeth of sharks and whales. The presence of soapstone (steatite) provides evidence that they traded with the Catalina Island tribes, as soapstone abounded there, while the lack of metals and glass indicates that they did not trade with Europeans or Asiatics.

One unfortunate footnote concerning our knowledge of the tribes who flourished in the Cambria area: In 1813, a Spanish law required the mission padres to record all the information they could gather about the pre-mission lives of local tribal members. Potentially a treasure trove of information, the mission padres recorded information colored by their perspective: They wrote that these tribes were slovenly, dirty, and unintelligent. Needless to say, this recorded information is of negligible value—and a wonderful opportunity to record and recapture tribal legends and mores was lost forever.

Despite these missionary records, enough evidence exists to allow experts to conclude that Cambria tribes were gentle, generous and peaceful, and that they lived simply. Their family bonds were strong and they exhibited great love and patience for their children. They were also noted for their extreme cleanliness in handling and preparing food and possessed an advanced knowledge of medicinal herbs. For entertainment, they enjoyed music and dance and had a passion for gambling.

Early Explorers

There is some evidence that a number of ships visited the area that would become Cambria. Some had drifted there on the Japanese or Alaskan currents. Others may have been Russian ships seeking otter.

The first recorded observations were provided in 1542 when **Juan Rodriguez Cabrillo** passed nearby on his fruitless search for a passage from the Pacific to the Atlantic. He recorded a deep indentation with a high, conical rock and named it "El Moro" (Morro Bay). Next he recorded a bay he called "Bay of Sardines," San Simeon Bay.

Although Cabrillo had claimed California for Spain in the 16th century, it was not until two centuries later that Spain began to exert control over the distant land. By that time, trade had become an important source of a nation's income, and it was evident that the country that controlled California's harbors would reap incredible profits. When England, France, and Russia began to covet California's coastline, Spain knew that it was time to assert its ownership.

The Spaniards planned to fortify the coast by building presidios (forts) and convert the natives by establishing missions. Before this could be accomplished, Spain needed to know more about this enormous, unexplored area. To gain first-hand information, an overland expedition of 67 men and 100 pack mules, led by **Gaspar de Portola**, left San Diego in 1769, heading for Monterey Bay. Progress was slow as the expedition had to wait for scouts to identify passable routes before proceeding.

This expedition provided a wealth of information. The recorder, **Father Juan Crespi**, gave us our first written description of the Cambria area and its local tribes. Camped at Santa Rosa Creek, near today's Coast Union High School, Crespi wrote:

> *. . . we discovered a mountainous region covered with pine and a canyon of great depth whose sides were thickly filled with trees. Pursuing our route (NNW) we encountered a large creek by whose banks we made a halt for the night, high above the canada. There came to visit us some 70 gentiles of a rancheria which was not far distant from us and they presented us with bowls of pinole for which we returned beads. They brought and offered us a bear cub, which they had bred up; but we refused it. From this circumstance, the soldiers took occasion to name the place Del Osito. I called it San Benvenuto.*

The Portola Expedition also provided what some experts believe to be evidence that the local tribes were migratory: When journeying north in the summer, they encountered tribes inland. Upon their return in the winter, they found that the tribes had settled along the shore.

Spanish Mission Society

Soon after Portola's reports of a lovely land populated with friendly tribes, Spain began building presidios and missions. Four presidios were built, first in Monterey and San Diego, with Santa Barbara and San Francisco following. While they were being built, missions were established to convert the tribes and cultivate the land. Each mission was given control of all surrounding land to ensure there would be plenty of space for the converted natives, called neophytes, to master agrarian skills. Spain also expected that the missions would use their vast expanses of land, with their free neophyte labor, to achieve self-sufficiency.

Almost overnight, most of these missions prospered until they were far better provisioned and more powerful than any of the presidios. Dominating all land and most of the resources of California, this mission society soon became the major economic and political force in California. The Spanish king had hoped that, as soon as the neophytes had been converted and had adopted European habits and skills, the mission lands would be returned to them and the missions would cease to exist. He had not anticipated the incredible power of these missions, nor had he anticipated the intense Church resistance to dissolving them.

Several missions were soon built in the area, including Mission San Luis Obispo de Tolosa and Mission San Miguel de Archangel in the Salinas Valley. The closest of these missions, San Luis Obispo, had minimal impact on Cambria. Instead, it was the more distant mission at San Miguel that was granted control of the area.

Despite this lack of direct impact on Cambria, establishment of the mission in San Luis Obispo had a major significance to the area that was to become San Luis Obispo County. This mission, established

September 1, 1772, was immediately successful converting the tribes. Beginning with fewer than 10 neophytes, in just over a decade, 616 had been baptized there. As a result of these neophytes' hard manual labor, many structures were soon completed, including a church, a hospital, a schoolhouse, and a nunnery for females awaiting marriage. Land was cultivated and, within a few years, vineyards and gardens flourished, while cattle, sheep, and horses roamed the vast expanses of land.

Before long, Mission San Luis Obispo had emerged as one of California's most prosperous and powerful missions. According to Colton, in *Three Years in California:*

> *In 1821 the mission of San Luis Obispo had 78,000 cattle, 2000 tame horses, 3700 mules and 2700 sheep. One of the fathers of this mission took $100,000 with him when he left for Spain in 1828.*

Mission San Luis Obispo padres routinely participated in a favorite illegal coastal activity: smuggling. Spain had imposed heavy taxes on all foreign ships, but had neither the resources nor inclination to enforce collection of these taxes. The traders wanted the hides and tallow of the Mission and needed the produce that abounded on Mission lands to replenish their dwindling supplies. On the other hand, the padres needed the tools and equipment Spain had promised but had not delivered. Wearied by waiting years for promised provisions and with more cattle and produce than they could use, the padres gladly traded with the smugglers. Soon a flourishing system of illegal trade was bringing ships to the area routinely.

In addition to needed tools and equipment, this trade provided the Mission with a variety of supplies, such as handkerchiefs, clothes, tobacco, and trinkets for the neophytes; religious ornaments; musical instruments; and books from England and the East. Smuggler ships also brought luxury items from China, such as silk, dishes, furniture, and chests covered with the tooled and dyed hides that had recently been obtained from the missions. Before long, Mission San Luis Obispo had exquisite gold religious furnishings, embroidered cloth, and all the equipment and tools the padres needed.

In 1779, when the second mission in the area, Mission San Miguel, was being built, the padres journeyed to the Cambria area seeking beams for their chapel. The cedar and pine from its forests were perfect, and neophytes from Mission San Miguel cleared a cart trail between San Miguel and San Simeon. Not only did the padres get the beams they needed, they also decided that they wanted to control this lovely land. They petitioned Spain for it, saying they needed more grazing land. In reality, they also wanted it so that they would have coastal access and could participate in the lucrative smuggling that had enriched Mission San Luis Obispo.

Their petition was granted, and Mission San Miguel soon controlled an enormous amount of land, including today's San Simeon and Cambria. Although the Mission radically changed the tribesmen's lives in the Salinas Valley, the impact on the tribes in Cambria was minimal. The padres' plan was to convert all local tribes before recruiting converts from outlying areas, such as Cambria. Before they were able to journey to Cambria to begin this conversion, Mexico had gained possession and the mission system was dismantled.

Although Cambria tribes were never the focus of conversion activities, they were impacted slightly when Mission neophytes journeyed to the Cambria area to supplement their food supply with shellfish and seafood and to retrieve cattle and sheep that had wandered there. As trails began to bring padres and neophytes to the Cambria area, local tribes moved into the hills. Later, as Mexicans began to ranch the land, followed by settlers, these tribes moved farther and farther inland.

Despite its control of an enormous amount of land, Mission San Miguel was never as prosperous as Mission San Luis Obispo. Where everything seemed to flourish in San Luis Obispo, the padres at San Miguel could not get their land to produce the fabulous fruits and vegetables growing in San Luis Obispo. So poor was their production that it is likely that, if the Mission San Luis Obispo padres had not given them food, there would have been seasons of extreme hunger and even starvation at San Miguel.

Mission Decline and Secularization

Mission San Luis Obispo caught fire three times and was attacked by the inland Tulare tribe. The fires and attack, although upsetting and causing damage that required hundreds of hours of neophyte labor to repair, did not significantly contribute to the Mission's decline. Rather, the cycle of disease and death among neophytes throughout California foretold the demise of the entire mission system. Without healthy neophytes able to do hard manual labor, missions could not survive.

In the early decades of the 19th century, those with foresight recognized that the neophytes were not thriving in the missions. Exposed to illness introduced by Russian otter hunters, the Spanish, and the continuous parade of smugglers, neophyte deaths increased, and birth rates plummeted. Although it took Mexico's victory over Spain and the secularization of all land to end the era of mission domination, the tragic decline of California tribes spelled the inevitable demise of this powerful institution.

When it became clear that Mexico was winning its war for independence from Spain and would soon own California, many wondered what changes Mexico would impose. Although Mexico won its independence and took possession of California in 1821, it was not until 1833 that the Mexican Congress had adopted a *Decree of Secularization*. This decree mandated that all missions be converted to parish churches and that the vast mission resources, except the church itself, be transferred to the government. Throughout California, padres were removed and replaced by curates. Although some vehemently opposed this decree, others, who had chafed under the unfairness of a society that had given the Church all the land, resources, and power, cheered the arrival of the Mexicans and the end of the mission system.

The huge tracts of land comprising the missions were dispersed. Although neophytes were given land, grain, cattle, and equipment, few were successful achieving self-sufficiency. Instead, most either sold their land or were cheated out of it and, before long, were either working for or had joined the Tulare tribe. During this transition, much that had been developed under the mission system disappeared. Before long, Mission San Miguel lay in ruins, Mission San Luis Obispo had been sold, huge herds ran wild, cultivated lands reverted to nature, and equipment had been stolen or left to rot.

Mexican Ranchos

As the missions were being dismantled, Mexicans saw a golden opportunity to acquire land, and many petitioned for it. Before long, huge tracts of land throughout California were awarded to loyal Mexican soldiers and citizens. Almost immediately, the power in California shifted from the padres to the rancheros (ranch owners) who had been given these land grants. Two who had proven their loyalty to the Mexican government, **Jose de Jesus Pico** and **Juliano Estrada**, were awarded land grants in the Cambria area.

In 1840, Jose de Jesus Pico, the cousin of the last Mexican governor, **Pio Pico**, was rewarded for his help overthrowing Spanish rule with an enormous land grant, the largest allowable under Mexican law. Named Rancho de la Piedra Blanca after the impressive rocks painted white by its huge bird population, it spanned 48,805 acres or 136 square miles, and included 14 miles of coastline extending from south of San Simeon to Ragged Point. As required by law, Pico built a dwelling, cultivated the land, and stocked it with animals. Having met the requirements, he left the rancho and only visited twice a year.

Instead, Pico took an active role in the political maneuverings that typified the era of Mexican rule. When he did come to the rancho, it was to participate in the activities that characterized this unique era, remembered as "Old California": roundups and matanzas (slaughterings) replete with vaqueros (cowboys), enormous amounts of food, gambling, horse racing, and, most important, wonderful music and dancing.

The era of Mexican rule was short-lived and, by the mid-1840s, it was clear to all that the United States would soon own California. Although savvy enough not to oppose the imminent American takeover, Pico was implicated in an 1846 conspiracy involving allegedly treasonable dispatches. He was arrested by **John C. Fremont** and sentenced to death at sunrise the next morning. According to one account, while Pico was awaiting death, his wife enlisted the help of her friends. These women came with their children, including all 14 of Pico's, begging, crying, praying, and wailing for his life to be spared. Wisely, the Americans released him. They knew he was less dangerous to them alive than as a martyred hero. They were right, and Pico soon became a positive political force in the new American territory, working successfully with Fremont.

Like Pico's Rancho de la Piedra Blanca, the other large land grant in the area, encompassing the Cambria area, was blessed with abundant water and wildlife. When Mexico began giving away land, this rich rancho was coveted. In 1838, Juliano Estrada petitioned the Governor for it and, by 1841, he had been officially awarded the 13,184-acre land grant called Rancho Santa Rosa. Like Pico, Estrada built his adobe and left it in the care of family members. Unlike Pico, by 1849, Estrada had brought his family to settle there. During the next decade, despite the daily hardships of life in a primitive land, he and his family basked in the Old California lifestyle of fancy clothes, fine horses and saddles, lavish barbecues, and frequent fiestas, with music and dancing.

In addition to these two enormous ranchos, in 1842, another **Estrada, Jose Ramon**, was granted almost 4500 acres wedged between Rancho de la Piedra Blanca and San Simeon Creek. Called Rancho San Simeon, Estrada sold it shortly before his death in 1845. Subsequently sold five times between 1845 and 1867, the rancho was eventually acquired by the Van Gordens, who became one of Cambria's important founding families.

Although these rancheros attempted to gain self-sufficiency by producing much of what they needed, they also enjoyed the extravagant clothing, jewelry, and saddles they acquired from smuggling. Under Spanish rule, all foreign ships had been heavily taxed. Under Mexican rule, laws were even more restrictive, and all trade with foreign ships was illegal. Although Spain could not enforce its taxation laws, Mexico was even less successful at excluding foreign ships from California's shores. Soon, the smuggling that had been prevalent in Spanish times became the dominant economic force under Mexican rule. Rancheros obtained everything they could not produce for themselves by trading hides, tallow, and produce to the grateful smugglers.

This lucrative trade allowed Pico and Estrada to barter their otherwise nearly valueless cattle for the extravagant clothing, jewelry, and fancy saddles they so loved. This trade also allowed them to indulge in their resplendent fiestas and lavish lifestyles. For those who participated in this festive and genteel world, it was a very good time and is remembered fondly. Despite the pleasantries of these days, Pico and Estrada knew that Mexico would not be able to control the promise-filled land for long. They knew it was only a matter of time before the United States would reach West for California. While they continued to party, they watched and they waited for the inevitable changes.

California Gold Rush

When America gained possession of California in 1846 through the *Treaty of Guadalupe-Hidalgo* that concluded the Mexican-American War, Pico and Estrada were not alone in wondering what changes the new government would bring. Accustomed to the neglect and disorganization of the Mexican government that had allowed them to function independently, many watched the Americans with concern.

At first, life under United States ownership improved significantly for Mexican rancheros. Cattle, initially valued only for hides and tallow, became an essential food source when gold was found in California in 1849. California's population skyrocketed during the Gold Rush, and gold-seeking prospectors were willing to pay dearly for the beef they craved. Almost overnight, the moderately lucrative hide and tallow trade was transformed into an extremely lucrative beef trade. Huge herds were driven to San Francisco, and wealth poured into the pockets of the rancheros.

The Gold Rush ushered in an era marked by prosperity (for the rancheros) and even more frequent genteel parties and lavish fiestas. Celebrants from neighboring ranchos arrived dressed in resplendent clothes and sporting elegant jewels and saddles. For just over a decade after the American takeover, life was very good for these Mexican land grantees, who continued to dominate the financial and social life of California. Although technically owned by America, life was much as it had been under Mexican rule, except that the good life was even better.

Breakup of the Ranchos

Changes began for the Mexican land grantees when, in the late 1850s, each ranchero was required to prove that they legally owned his rancho. This proof required a survey confirming the original survey and, usually, legal help to file petitions. To their horror, surveyors and lawyers demanded cash. Known for lavish and generous spending, most rancheros used a barter system and simply did not have the cash required. Many were forced to borrow money to pay these fees.

When the survey of Rancho Santa Rosa was complete in 1858, Estrada learned that his rancho spanned 13,184 acres. He also learned that he owed $7900 for this survey and legal fees. He agreed to the loan offered by a young, handsome, wealthy lawyer who had recently emigrated from Spain to California, **Domingo Pujol**. This loan required a 2% compounded monthly interest rate that translated to a whopping 27% per year. As he had no way to pay the debt and had used his entire rancho as collateral for the loan, foreclosure proceedings began within nine months. When it was over eight years later, Estrada held only the 1500 acres that surrounded his home, while Pujol owned the rest of the huge rancho.

On top of the devastating fees, in 1863, the first of a series of severe droughts swept the region. Cattle by the thousands congregated around disappearing creeks and slowly perished from starvation. The land had become so dry that grass simply could not grow. When it was clear to Pico that there was no hope for his cattle, he killed them by driving them off a cliff as a kinder alternative to the slow starvation they were destined to suffer. After three successive drought seasons, leaving the land strewn with dead cattle, it was clear that the days of the large, prosperous ranchos had ended. By the time the rains came back, only a few cattle had survived. The enormous losses resulting from the death of their cattle, combined with high survey and legal debts, resulted in the breakup of these huge land grants. Pico and Estrada watched stoically as their lavish life of comfort, respectability, influence, and affluence disappeared forever.

By 1866, both Estrada and Pico, despite having proven their legal ownership of their ranchos, had lost them. When this happened, the best land on California's Central Coast was suddenly available to anyone with vision and money. The breakup of these two huge ranchos, plus the earlier sale in 1845 of Rancho San Simeon, provided the opportunity for ranchers, entrepreneurs, and speculators to buy land—and heralded the birth of Cambria.

Arrival of the Hearsts

George Hearst had both the vision and the money to take advantage of the breakup of these ranchos. Hearst had been born in Missouri in 1820 to farmers, and had decided early that farming was too hard and not profitable enough. By 1850, he had joined the California Gold Rush. He prospected unsuccessfully for the next 10 years, until he hit a bonanza in 1859 by buying a one-sixth interest in the Ophir silver mine, part of the rich Comstock Lode. After this windfall, this mining genius successfully invested in a variety of silver, gold, and copper mines.

By the time his only child, **William Randolph**, was born in 1863, Hearst had also developed an interest in real estate. He found the perfect combination of these interests, land, and potentially valuable mines, when he discovered the San Simeon region. Not only did he envision San Simeon Bay as an important port, he was also intrigued by the discovery of quicksilver in the area. He moved quickly to acquire all the available land and to develop the lovely bay.

He had competition for this land, as he was not the first to settle in the San Simeon area. When he came in 1865 and began buying Pico's Rancho de la Piedra Blanca, 17,000 acres of the rancho had already been sold to settlers. Other settlers had begun ranching on public domain land they had purchased for $1.25 an acre, while yet another group had illegally squatted on portions of the rancho. Hearst's first step toward acquiring San Simeon was to purchase 30,000 acres of Rancho de la Piedra Blanca. He then began a decades-long tradition of buying plots whenever they became available until he and his family had amassed much of San Simeon.

Hearst also began to strategize the acquisition of surrounding land. He wanted to buy the land at the junction of the trails along Santa Rosa Creek and the coast, the future location of Cambria. This land, part of Estrada's Santa Rosa Rancho, was not for sale, as Pujol was in the process of repossessing it. Nevertheless, while Pujol was foreclosing on Rancho Santa Rosa, George Hearst purchased it from Estrada in an amazingly good deal – $3000. The deed gave Hearst 13,024 acres and left 160 acres for Estrada.

Unfortunately for Hearst, Estrada did not have the right to sell this land, and Hearst did not discover this until the deed had been recorded and the money paid. After three trips to court, he realized that he would not win and walked away with nothing. When Pujol's repossession was complete and Estrada was left with only 1500 acres, he sold 1340 of these acres to Hearst. In the space of a few years, Estrada's holdings had shrunk from 13,184 acres to a mere 160 acres, while Hearst's and Pujol's had grown enormously.

When Estrada died in 1871, his 17 year old son, **Francisco "Poncho"**, took over the management of his remaining 160 acres and provided a home for his mother and siblings. When they left in 1876, they sold their 160 acres to Hearst who then hired "Poncho" who worked on Hearst's San Simeon ranch the rest of his life. Estrada's adobe was torn down by the Hearsts, but when Highway 1 was widened, residents of Cambria salvaged a number of artifacts from the ruins of his old adobe, including pottery, a candleholder, and some roof tiles.

In 1866, as soon as the title to Santa Rosa Rancho had been cleared and Pujol owned the land, he divided it up and offered it for sale. **John Myers** and **William Gillespie** were his first customers. They bought 195 acres north of Cambria. Not surprisingly, Hearst was also one of Pujol's early customers. By 1868, Hearst had bought a number of Pujol's plots, until he owned 3000 acres of the original Rancho Santa Rosa, in addition to his San Simeon holdings.

The breakup of these two ranchos spurred the arrival of settlers and entrepreneurs, and set the stage for the establishment of Cambria. Before Cambria was Cambria, it was the home to local tribes, part of the enormous Mission San Miguel lands, awarded as a Mexican land grant, and was actively sought by many when it was dissolved. Once ruled by Spain and Mexico, it was now part of a new American state and on the verge of becoming a vibrant and hopeful new town.

Early Cambria, known as 'Slab Town'

A Town Is Born, 1866-1872

In 1850, when San Luis Obispo County was organized as one of California's original counties, it was an enormous, sparsely settled county encompassing 1.5 million acres. Its only settlement of any size was San Luis Obispo, with a population of 1000. Fifteen years later, at the end of the Civil War in 1865, a long parade of settlers began trekking West seeking new homes. These settlers sought a mild climate and inexpensive land with good soil, streams, and lumber. Available land seldom offered all these amenities. Land in the area that was to become Cambria had fertile land, streams, and virgin pine forests and was, for many, a dream come true.

Settlers first looked for free or inexpensive government land. The lucky ones found some and began to cultivate it. **Jeffrey Phelan** was among the first of many to arrive to settle in this lovely and lush coastal area by acquiring government land to cultivate. Originally from Waterford, Ireland, he arrived in the area in 1857, soon after the completion of the survey of Rancho de la Piedra Blanca. He was able to purchase 160 acres of unclaimed government land two miles north of Cambria. Laws gave land to those who promised to build schools, so Phelan soon acquired an additional 320 acres and built Cambria's first school. In addition to his dairying and school-building activities, he is credited with providing the site (for $100) for today's landmark Santa Rosa Chapel, and allowing seasonal use of his land for a community picnic area/rodeo grounds, known as "Phelan's Grove."

William Leffingwell was another one of the lucky ones who found unclaimed government land. In 1859, he brought his wife and some of his seven adult children to settle on public lands adjacent to Rancho de la Piedra Blanca. As soon as he had secured the land by building a home, cultivating the land, and stocking it, he acquired some coastal land at the north end of Moonstone Beach. He established several businesses there, including a lumber mill, a forge, a landing and, eventually, a wharf.

Those who could not identify government land, but who had some money, purchased plots as soon as the huge land grants were subdivided and offered for sale. Within a decade, the land on which wild Mexican cattle had roamed was dotted with neat farms. According to Myron Angel's 1883 *History of San Luis Obispo County:*

> *Here, in this favored spot, began to rise the household fires of a new population. From every civilized quarter of the earth's broad surface came one or more to help build up a new community, and their efforts succeeded. Upon the fertile waste, where but lately roamed the wild manada (undomesticated horses), now thrifty farmers . . . live, and business thrives apace.*

While settlers in other regions had to buy lumber or learn to love adobe dwellings, Cambria settlers were blessed with plentiful pine. Soon buildings constructed of rough pine, with bark still attached, were so prevalent that early Cambria was disdainfully called "Slab Town," the first of its many names. Unfortunately, though cheap and convenient, this pine tended to rot far more easily than harder woods, such as redwood and fir.

The first industries in the area were lumbering and land speculation. John Myers and William Gillespie, Pujol's first customers when he subdivided Rancho Santa Rosa, pursued both of these industries. They purchased 195 acres of heavily timbered land on the northwest corner of the rancho in 1866 and established a sawmill. They cleared the land to increase its value, offered it for sale, and then sold the lumber from the land back to the settlers. They were successful and, within three months, Myers and Gillespie had sold all their land. They then sold their mill to **F. F. Letcher** and **J. W. Ford.**

While most came to ranch, a variety of entrepreneurs followed and opened service and supply enterprises to support them. The small stretch of level land at the junction of the private road serving upper Santa Rosa Creek and the coastal route from San Luis Obispo was the natural choice for these businesses. The first to settle there, in 1865, was **Philip Kaetzel**, a skilled wheelwright, who was lucky enough to identify 160 acres of unclaimed government land at this junction. Convinced that he had found the perfect location for a thriving community, he built a home, acquired some cattle, established a business as a wheelwright, and waited for others to arrive.

He was right. Before long, entrepreneurs **George Grant** and **George Lull** arrived. They wanted to lease a small portion of Kaetzel's land along Santa Rosa Creek, with an option to buy. Grant, the financier, returned to San Francisco, while Lull remained to establish a business and seek local investors. By 1865, Lull had found local investors, purchased the land, and completed a small two-story building near what was to become downtown Cambria. Grant, Lull and Company, a general merchandise store, was on the ground floor, while his home was on the second floor.

By October 1866, the adjacent land was subdivided and offered for sale when speculators **George Long** and **Samuel Pollard** purchased just over 2000 acres from Pujol and divided it into smaller parcels to sell. Although Pollard lived in San Luis Obispo, he kept enough of this land to build a general store that competed with Grant and Lull's store. Long and Pollard sold 150 of their acres to **Rufus Rigdon**, who brought his family and became Cambria's notary and justice of the peace. **George Proctor**, a blacksmith and **George Davis**, an engineer, also purchased land from Long and Pollard. They established the town's first hotel, The Davis House, later enlarged to become the county's first three-story building and renamed the Proctor House. Proctor continued to buy land until he owned many lots, as evidenced by the frequency his name appears in town records as the early owner of key downtown buildings.

These downtown land acquisitions by Kaetzel, Lull, Long, Pollard, Rigdon, Proctor, and Davis—Cambria's founding fathers — established the roots of a promising new town. Downtown streets were platted, businesses opened, and it was clear that enthusiasm for the young town was growing rapidly. By the end of 1866, they united, calling themselves "the Citizens of Santa Rosa," when they petitioned the San Luis Obispo Board of Supervisors for better roads. This began the first of many transportation battles they would wage –and established a long-standing tradition of community involvement with the Supervisors.

New England Look-Alike

The settlement immediately became the focal point of the area by supplying services and products to the outlying mines and ranches. It was also the social and political center of the region, replete with the largest assembly hall in the county. A livery stable opened, a second wheelwright arrived, several new stores were established, and, before long, Cambria could offer the services of a carriagemaker, a shoemaker, and a doctor, who also served as the local news correspondent for the *San Luis Obispo Tribune*.

As the town grew, property gained value, and lots were divided and subdivided. Before long, downtown lots had been divided so often that they were only 25 by 50 feet. An engineer, **Peter A. Forrester**, the son-in-law of ranchero Jose Pico, and the man who suggested the name "Cambria," surveyed the town. Referred to as "Forrester's Plat," this survey established Cambria's legal boundaries. Unfortunately, "Forrester's Plat" was destined to be incorrect, for it used Santa Rosa Creek as the boundary of many lots. As the creek changed course, the survey was rendered inaccurate. As a result, in subsequent years, many owners were disappointed to find that the property they thought they owned differed markedly from its legal boundaries.

Very different from California's more traditional Spanish-style adobe settlements, Cambria, with its wooden buildings, looked more like New England than California. According to the August 14, 1869 *San Luis Obispo Tribune:*

> *We have two towns in our flourishing county, each the antipodes of the other. One, San Luis Obispo with its old mission building and church, and its prevailing adobe style of architecture reminds us of the past–slow but solid.*
>
> *Cambria with its brand new brightness, and its rapid growth, marks the advancement hither of American improvement. Three years ago the name of Cambria was unknown to the county; not a house stood where now here can be collected together on any important occasion, an assembly of one thousand souls; and only Nature's sounds were heard, where now the air resounds with the whir of the steam-saw, the heavy pounding of the blacksmith's*

sledge, and the brisker tappings of the carpenter's hammer. . . . It can boast today of one first class country hotel and several restaurants of a less imposing appearance.

During these early years, many settlers turned to dairying as their focus, and Cambria was soon supporting large and productive dairy farms. On the way to replacing lumber and land sales as Cambria's premier industry, by 1869, the San Luis Obispo Board of Equalization ordered that all property be assessed using the following values:

American milch cows. . . . .$25 each
Stock cattle. . . . . $15 each
Mixed dairy cows. $22.50
Spanish dairy cows. $20
American work horses. $45
Spanish work horses. $25
Sheep, first class. $2
Sheep, fourth class. $1

By 1869, Cambria had emerged as a promising town with untold potential for growth. Citizens knew that it was only a matter of time before Cambria would outgrow other towns to become the second largest in the county.

Great Name Debate

Despite all this progress, Cambria had one problem: it had no name. On October 2, 1867, a Post Office was established in the Grant, Lull and Company's second store at the southwest corner of Main and Bridge Streets. Required by the Post Office to submit three names, citizens selected Santa Rosa, Rosaville, and San Simeon. Expecting to be assigned one of their first choices, Santa Rosa or Rosaville, they were dismayed to be assigned San Simeon as their official name. They all knew that Hearst's settlement 8 miles to the north had already unofficially claimed that name.

At that time, George Hearst was busy subdividing his San Simeon lots and applying for a franchise to build a pier there. Watching his progress, citizens knew that they could not share their name with him, but made no progress in agreeing on another name. Before long, Hearst and his partner, **Captain Joseph Clark**, a whaler from the Azores, who ran the San Simeon Whaling Station , were granted permission to build a wharf. By the summer of 1869, their pier was under construction, and the pressure to agree on a new name was high.

A meeting was called and the commitment was made that the meeting would not adjourn until consensus on a name had been reached. The meeting went on and on into the night. Finally, when all were tired and frustrated, Peter Forrester, the town's surveyor and engineer, casually suggested the name of "Cambria," after the city in Pennsylvania. After a very brief discussion, the name was endorsed. Derived from the Latin word for Wales, the new name surprised many. Myron Angel, in his 1883 *History of San Luis Obispo County*, captured some of the amused and bemused reactions to the town's new name:

> *Its derivation is obvious, but its application incomprehensible. To a town full of Welshmen, it might seem applicable, but to a place mostly made up of American people, and presumably of the severely practical and unimaginative sort, it would seem an unmeaning designation.*

Despite this reaction, on January 10, 1870, the Post Office officially accepted the name change, and the young town finally had a name.

Transportation Challenges

For years, many believed that a major seaport could thrive in the area, and most recognized that San Simeon was the logical location for this port. Having been used by smugglers during Spanish and Mexican years, entrepreneurs predicted dramatically increased commercial activity as the population swelled. Leffingwell Landing, although closer and more convenient, was less protected and, without a wharf, its utility was limited, for everything had to be rowed or floated in over the surf. When Hearst and Clark partnered to build their wharf at San Simeon, the days when the landing could compete with the wharf were numbered.

What residents had not bargained for was Hearst's charges. When the wharf was completed in 1869, Hearst began collecting fees for everything brought to or taken from San Simeon Bay. Some tried to avoid these charges by going over the beach. Although a rough and difficult way to get to the wharf, it worked for too many, and Hearst decided that it must stop. To accomplish this, he began proceedings in 1870 to secure title to the tidelands at San Simeon. By 1871, he had been awarded control of 100 acres of tidelands for $1 an acre under the Tidelands Act. He was now able to legally control the movement of all goods on the bay's sandy beach and raise rates at will. Most area settlers paid Hearst's continually accelerating wharfage. Their only other choices were rowing freight ashore at Leffingwell's, or transporting goods by road to other more distant wharfs, such as Cayucos.

Despite the wet landings at Leffingwell's and the rising costs at San Simeon, the sea continued to offer the only efficient form of transporting goods in and out of Cambria for many years. Those who had to travel by land to San Luis Obispo, or another more distant wharf, faced a rough and tedious journey. Despite the difficulties, stagecoach service to San Luis Obispo came early to Cambria. By 1867, stages regularly served Cambria and, by 1869, stagecoach travel was available every Monday, Wednesday, and Friday for $3 each way for

Off-loading Lumber at Leffingwell Landing

Hearst's Pier, 1880s

passengers and additional charges for freight. Leaving at 7 a.m. from Cambria, it was due to arrive in San Luis Obispo by 3 p.m. In the summer months, though deep ruts and thick dust abounded, the stage usually took 8 to 9 hours and arrived close to the scheduled time. In the winter, however, mud and floods could completely prevent travel or prolong the journey to 12 or more hours.

Quicksilver!

Although its fertile land, streams, and lumber would draw settlers to the area, it was the whispered tales of riches in the hills that turned the small settlement into a boomtown. Fueling these rumors was the 1862 discovery of cinnabar, the mineral in which quicksilver (mercury) is found, in the headwaters of Santa Rosa Creek. Many of the local settlers were 1849 Gold Rush prospectors-turned-farmers, so mining fever was easily re-sparked. The timing for this discovery was good as the Civil War raged in the East. Wartime needs had increased both the price and demand for mercury, used to process the silver that financed the Union Army and also used in the percussion caps for soldiers' rifles. Adding to the excitement was the discovery of smaller veins of gold and copper.

By January 1864, 40 Californios (descendents of the Spanish and Mexican-era settlers in California) and American hopefuls had incorporated to form the Josephine Quicksilver Mining District. Many acquired a share of this promising mine, among them, partners **C. B. Rutherford** and **Walter Murray**. Within a few years it became clear that little progress was being made and Rutherford and Murray decided to take action. Rutherford went to San Francisco to raise money by selling shares, many of which neither he nor Murray owned. He was successful and sold a majority of the Josephine Quicksilver Mining District shares for $25,000, also negotiating an additional bonus of $20,000 for himself and Murray.

Before that illegal deal could be completed, word leaked out, and the large San Francisco-based Bolton, Barron, & Company cut them out by purchasing a controlling interest. When Bolton, Barron, & Company acquired ownership of the Josephine Mine in 1867, things began to happen, and, in the next three years, the company shipped $280,000 worth of quicksilver out of San Simeon. In the midst of the boom, while prices were still high, the Josephine began to experience hard times and, by 1874, production had dwindled. Owners were forced to dig more expensive tunnels. Before long, these tunnels had cost $100,000, but had yielded no rich veins. In desperation, Bolton, Baron and Company tried unsuccessfully to acquire other more profitable mines to offset their losses. Surrounded by profitable mines, the Josephine languished.

In 1871, when **Orzo Haskins** was looking for a sawmill site in Pine Mountain, eight miles north of the Josephine Mine and 11 miles from Cambria, he found a sample rich with mercury. According to the November 18, 1871 edition of the *San Luis Obispo Tribune:*

> *Our neighbors in the usually quiet town of Cambria are in the midst of an intense mining excitement. . . . Last week (Haskins) . . . returned to town with quite a large number of rich specimens. His discovery created a furor, and a rush was incontinently made to the Pine Bluffs, and locations have been staked out all along the line of the lead for a great distance.*

Today (Saturday) there will be a meeting in Cambria for the purpose of organizing a mining district, and adopting such laws and rules and regulations as are usual in like cases. By the next steamer, a trusty agent will be dispatched to San Francisco with samples of the ore for thorough assay, and arrangements [for] machinery and retorts. . . . Quicksilver prospects in our county are certainly looking up finely.

Almost immediately, more than 150 claims were filed. Intense mining operations began, and results were promising, yielding 2-8% quicksilver. Despite these promising yields, Pine Mountain claim holders faced challenges. Haskins was never successful. He bonded and rebonded his claim and allowed his mines to be mismanaged. Eventually, all his bonds had to be surrendered. Two other Pine Mountain claimholders were also unsuccessful: They invested more than $200,000 in machinery and a furnace but, due to a drop in quicksilver prices, were forced to offer their claim for $70,000.

Others were more successful. Owners of the Keystone Mine worked for three years to install furnaces and condensers. When they finally began mining operations in 1874, this mine became the first Pine Mountain claim to be profitable. It was sold in 1874 for $22,000. Soon afterward, a much larger and richer vein was discovered, and it was mined whenever mercury prices rose.

The Oceanic

Closer to Cambria, three-quarters of a mile north of Santa Rosa Creek and five miles from downtown, **Ben Phillips** and **George Morss** discovered a rich lode in 1872 when a horse kicked up a rock with bright red streaks. Knowing these streaks indicated cinnabar, they staked a claim immediately. Other claims followed.

By 1874, these claims were sold for $36,000 to San Francisco capitalists, who formed the Oceanic Quicksilver Mining Company. Capital stock was fixed at $6 million and 60,000 shares at $25 a share were offered. Owners worked to expand their claim by buying adjacent property, or trading Oceanic stock to acquire surrounding land. A number of landowners were willing to sell or trade and, before long, the boundaries of the claim had been significantly expanded. Employing 300, it was soon the biggest quicksilver mine in the area.

No expense was spared on the Oceanic—hoped to be the richest quicksilver mine on the continent. (Although it never surpassed production of the New Alameden in Santa Clara, it did become the 6th largest quicksilver mine in the world.) Three furnaces of the latest, most modern design were built, and 7 tunnels were completed. Stock prices jumped to $30 per share, and hopes were high. At that time, mercury prices were still good, the mine was relatively easy to work, and the quality of the ore was high. Cambrians dreamed of the many ways they would spend the fortunes they were about to make. Unfortunately, soon after the Oceanic began to produce significant quantities, the price of mercury had fallen, and Cambria's first quicksilver boom was over.

By 1878, with expenditures high and mercury prices falling, the once-profitable Oceanic had amassed judgments against it that totaled $110,000. Although the owners continued to manage the mine, the property, mineral rights, and equipment were sold to the Bank of San Francisco for $50,000. By 1901, the Oceanic had accumulated enough capital to buy back the mineral rights and equipment from the bank. It produced well until 1908, when the ore petered out, and mining stopped until prices began to go up. By 1914, full operations began again and employment reached between 60 and 70 young Cambria men and 200 Chinese laborers who worked as miners, cooks, and general laborers. By December 1918, many new tunnels had been completed, but their cost challenged the financial well-being of the mine. With World War I drawing to a close and mercury prices falling, within a year, it had closed once again.

Booms

Cambria's mining history is characterized by cycles of prosperity and poverty, as mercury prices and production fluctuated wildly. Unlike some more easily mined minerals, quicksilver mining was expensive, requiring extensive tunneling and furnaces, and could not withstand price declines. During a boom in 1876, $282,832 in quicksilver was produced; four years later, production totaled only $6760 in value. Although mining came to a virtual standstill from 1888 until 1900, many abandoned mines were reopened between 1901 and 1918 when prices rose. As recently as 1963, another mining flurry began when prices for quicksilver reached almost $12 per pound. Today, the flamboyant dreams of mineral wealth that swept the area are only distant memories.

During boom times, Cambria grew and prospered by providing supplies and entertainment to the miners, many of whom were earning as much as $5 a day. These mining years accelerated Cambria's growth enormously. The population swelled during boom times. When the mines closed, many who had come to work in them found other occupations and stayed.

Those who predicted that Cambria's future would be to support the mines were wrong. Instead, as each boom faded, residents again focused their attention on establishing a vibrant supply and service center and a good place to live. They were successful, and, before long, many would agree with a visitor who described Cambria as: "A very American looking town, and her people have a brisk, pushing appearance. The stores and storekeepers look busy and prosperous; the houses have a neat New England appearance."

Days of Growth and Prosperity, 1872-1894

During the 1870s, Cambria experienced steady growth due to its role as the region's agricultural supply center as well as the influx of miners during boom years. Immigrants included Welsh and Chinese miners, Swiss-Italian dairymen, and an increased number of Mexican laborers. Unsurprisingly, these residents added a new element to the young town. By the late 1870s, Cambria's regional population had swelled to over 1000, including 300 living in or near downtown Cambria and another 300 employed in the thriving quicksilver mines.

Enthusiasm for growth was high, and many believed that Cambria was entering an era of growth, wealth, and importance. There was an air of energy and anticipation permeating the new young town. Its downtown was vibrant with new shops opening, customers with money, wagons hauling supplies to the mines, and hogs and cattle being driven to market.

Although most embraced the exciting new Cambria, some were concerned about the roughness this growth brought to their quiet town. Some, like **George Lingo**, decided to leave. In July 1875, a miner, named **E. Peter Smith**, who was staying at Lingo's hotel, the Cosmopolitan, disappeared without a trace, leaving all his belongings in his room. This was of such concern to Lingo that he sold the hotel and moved to San Luis Obispo, saying that Cambria had become too rough for him and his three teenage daughters. Leading citizen Peter Forrester, the engineer who had platted Cambria's streets, suggested its name, and grown wealthy from its mines, also moved to San Luis Obispo, where he became mayor and was eventually appointed State Commissioner of Immigration.

Even more disturbing than losing important citizens to San Luis Obispo was when **George Rothschild**, a partner in one of Cambria's general stores, located where Camozzi's Saloon is today, committed suicide in December 1873, soon after marrying and opening his new store. He left his grieving, pregnant wife, a saddened partner, **Abram Gans**, and shaken Cambrians who had grown fond of him.

But, for most, Cambria's boom years were wondrous—vibrant with purposeful people, interesting new buildings, well-stocked stores, and money to spend. When George Proctor expanded his hotel, renamed the Proctor Hotel, Cambria citizens boasted about their fine three-story building, the first in the entire county. By 1880, Cambria had amassed an impressive array of businesses and services. According to Myron Angel's 1883 *History of San Luis Obispo County*, these included:

> *. . . four general stores, two doctors, a dentist, a lawyer, three blacksmiths, several carriage shops, a Wells Fargo office, Western Union office, five saloons, a good three-story hotel, a wide variety of general retail stores, two drug stores, a saddlery and harness business, one furniture store, a butcher shop, a shoe repair, two livery stables, one jewelry store, a woman's dress shop, two wagon shops, two blacksmiths, a physician, a sawmill, an attorney, two churches, a public assembly hall, and a district schoolhouse with 100 students.*

Almost a Vibrant Seaport

Before the arrival of the railroad, ships provided the best and most convenient mode of travel up and down California's coast. Towns all along the coast envisioned their bays as the commercial centers of California and made great efforts to make their vision a reality. Cambria was no different, and leading citizens believed that, if a strong wharf could be built nearby, their town would become an affluent and influential seaport. Although Hearst's wharf at San Simeon accommodated ships and had steamer service to San Francisco three times a week, San Simeon was too distant and expensive to satisfy Cambrians. As Cambria grew, many wished for a closer seaport.

It appeared that this dream would come true in 1874, when William Leffingwell began building a wharf at his cove. For years, he had operated a landing at the end of today's Moonstone Beach that had provided a fair weather option for ships. Ships would anchor offshore and float most supplies in barrels ashore, while rowboats brought passengers and other items to shore, too often dumping them in the surf while landing. Despite the proximity of the landing, this inconvenience had always limited the utility of Leffingwell Landing. The building of this much-needed wharf progressed well, and by August 1874, Leffingwell and his sons had completed their wharf and welcomed their first schooner with speeches and a barbecue. Schooner passengers and Cambrians then went fishing together on San Simeon Creek, an expedition remembered for its many bites – unfortunately more from mosquitoes than trout!

It soon became clear that the wharf was too short for the cove's shallow water. Extending 300 feet into the sea, at low tide, it only reached a depth of 13 feet. Leffingwell knew that it had to be extended to deep water if it were to accommodate ships. By 1875, it had been extended an additional 100 feet and could accommodate the steamers that were regularly traveling up and down California's coast. Finally, Cambrians had much to celebrate, for they finally had both a convenient seaport and an economical alternative to Hearst's increasing rates at San Simeon.

Meanwhile, the wharf at San Simeon was being improved. Although it was still well used, its unsafe reputation, due to frequent heavy swells, was growing. This reputation was worrisome to Hearst, who counted on the wharf to support vibrant trade. He applied for, and was awarded, another franchise to improve his wharf. By 1878, he had built a 20-foot wide, 750-foot long wharf, replete with rails, and a 48′ by 100′ warehouse at a cost of $20,000 that was considered the finest in the county. By November 1880, the Board of Supervisors had fixed San Simeon wharfage rates at:

Merchandise, per ton $1
Lumber, per 1000 . . . . $1
Posts, per 100 . . . . $1
Wool, per ton $1
Eggs, per box of 30 dozen . . . . 16 cents
Livestock . . . . 12.5 cents

Cambria citizens' joy at the completion of a wharf at Leffingwell's was short-lived. Despite the convenience of this wharf, the cove was still a shallow, unprotected bay littered with dangerous rocks and known for a furious surf. In 1894, the schooner ***Electra*** was blown onto the rocks near the wharf and was a total loss. Captains were unwilling to take this risk, and the ***Electra*** was the last ship to use Leffingwell's wharf. By 1900, the wharf was gone. Cambrians, disappointed at the failure of their wharf, were forced to recognize that San Simeon was the only viable local seaport. This dependence on San Simeon continued until the railroad came to San Luis Obispo in 1894, forever changing coastal shipping.

Leading Citizens

Elmer Scott Rigdon, the son of Rufus Rigdon, one of Cambria's founding fathers, was born in Cambria in 1868 and symbolized a new generation of prosperous and politically savvy individuals who emerged during those vibrant years. Rigdon was a successful businessman who owned a number of downtown buildings, mining

Electra on the Rocks, 1894

partnerships, and a large amount of property in the northwest portion of Cambria.

When he realized that the bricks needed to build the retorts for processing cinnabar were being shipped all the way from San Luis Obispo, an eight-hour journey on the best of days, he began his own brickyard. He hired Chinese workers who had come to San Luis Obispo in 1894 to build the Southern Pacific Railroad and had been laid off when the work was done. Although his bricks were rumored to be of inferior quality, his influence and prestige swayed many to use them. Although a successful businessman, his passion was debate, and the life of a politician fit him well. In later years, he served as State Assemblyman and is credited with convincing the California Legislature to construct the Big Sur portion of Highway 1, recognized by many as the nation's most scenic roadway.

While Rigdon was known as Cambria's most persuasive orator and politician, George Lull, owner of Cambria's first general store, was noted for his impeccable clothes, dignity, and wealth – plus his intriguing status as the town's handsome and most eligible bachelor. His courtship of **Mary Leah Inman** has become one of Cambria's legends in which truth and fable intertwine. Many believe the legend that Lull purchased Mary from a man passing through town. When *The Cambrian* published this story in its June 15, 1989 edition, the response was almost immediate. By June 22, Mary's step great-granddaughter charged that the story was insulting and demanded an immediate retraction. In the June 29, 1989 *The Cambrian*, she wrote the true Mary Inman Lull story:

According to her, Mary was married to a professional gambler and traveled from the East Coast in a covered wagon with him. Eventually, she decided that she could no longer live the itinerant life of the wife of a professional gambler. Her husband left first and took their oldest daughter with him. Distraught, Mary began searching for her husband and daughter in one gambling-rich mining town after another. Finally, she found her daughter in Cambria "playing in the dirt with lice in her hair." Lull's step great-granddaughter did not know what happened next.

George Lull's Store, 1879

Without further evidence one can only surmise that . . . Lull, having seen and fallen for Mary, intervened to convince her husband to leave the girls and his wife and to move on. To move on, Inman just may have needed traveling money. How easy it would have been for Lull, the wealthy owner of the leading general store, to give him the clothes, boots, and even the money he needed to leave quickly on his journey, seeking promising gambling tables.

George and Mary lived together happily for many years. George built Mary a lovely home that was Cambria's largest, and considered pretentious by some, where they lived for many years. Later, in the 1930s, accommodations for the motorists who began to come to Cambria were built around this home, and it opened as Cambria's first tourist court, the Bluebird Motel, still one of Cambria's most popular places to stay. According to owners and confirmed by psychics, the gentle spirit of Mary still resides at the Bluebird.

One footnote to Lull's story: **George**, the son of one of Mary's daughters, gave the aging Lull a great deal of trouble and heartache. When Lull died in 1899, the 21 year old George was shocked to learn that he had been left only $1. A December 1899 *San Luis*

Obispo Tribune story may shed some light on his step-grandfather's disappointment and his surprising will:

> *Elizabeth Ann Blake, of Cambria, who charged George L. Lull with seduction under the promise of marriage, has brought suit to have the will of the late George W. Lull, heretofor admitted to probate, adjudged invalid. George L. Lull is the adopted son of the late George W. Lull, and the young man was a defendant in a damage suit some years since brought against him by Elizabeth Ann Blake. In this case, Miss Blake secured a judgment of $5000, which was never paid, and which she now seeks to compel payment by breaking the will of the late George W. Lull.*

Son George left Stanford University to become a soldier and fought well in the Philippines. He became a prominent San Luis Obispo attorney and, eventually, a District Attorney in San Francisco. Despite this success, Lull's fears for him were probably insightful, as George died before his time of alcoholism.

Entertainment

During these boom years, Cambria's long tradition of social organizations and celebrations was established. Masons, Odd Fellows, and Hesperian lodges were organized and flourished. By 1878, the Hesperians had accumulated the amazingly large treasury of $4000.

At the peak of prosperity, many Cambrians had considerable wealth. They found that the best way to spend an exciting afternoon, with the enticing chance of winning money, was at Cambria's increasingly popular Sunday horse races. Soon, the Cambria Jockey Club was organized and offered large purses of $100 to $150. So popular were these races that they soon became a region-wide passion. On December 12, 1874, the first trotting race was held in Cambria, and was attended by competitors from all over the county. The fever to win grew to such proportions that, by 1875, one rancher, **William DeNise**, had built himself a private half-mile race course so he could train for these races. By 1875, Cambria's races were considered the best in the county.

In addition to these races, Cambria citizens also participated in other festivities in Phelan's Grove. They consisted of barbecues, contests, sports, music, and dancing, and were the forerunners of decades of celebrations that have solidified Cambria's reputation as the premier host in the region.

Main Street, 1885

Pastimes other than these races and festivities often took place in one of Cambria's ever-present saloons. According to the *San Luis Obispo Tribune* in January 1892: "The boys often get together in some saloon and whistle, dance and sing. We see no disgrace in that, there is no other place to go unless you go to bed." By June 1899, the *Tribune* was glad to announce, "There has been another little enterprise started here in the way of an ice cream parlor. The public can now get ice cream every Saturday at the principal meat market." During these years full of the promise of ever-increasing mineral wealth, flourishing dairies, committed entrepreneurs, and great Sunday horse races, life was good. There was no stopping Cambria.

Unfortunately, they were soon to find out how vulnerable their new town was.

Fire!

This placid, prosperous period in Cambria's history was marked by violence when, in the early hours of October 1, 1889, a fire destroyed virtually all buildings in downtown Cambria. According to the *San Luis Obispo Tribune*:

> *At 2:30 this morning a fire started at the Proctor Hotel. The cause is unknown but the flames spread rapidly and in a half an hour the entire block was a mass of fire. The little water obtainable was of no service and there was no means of arresting the flames. Building after building caught, and in spite of all the efforts that could be made the destruction went on until there was nothing left within reach that could be consumed. Not even a shed is left. All the business portion of Cambria is wiped out. The buildings being entirely of wood the destruction was so rapid that there was not even the time to get out the contents of the stores or buildings. Hardly anything is saved and the town is destitute.*

Tragically, a 6000-gallon water tank close to the fire remained unused because the only way to access this water was by using a damaged garden hose at a single spigot at the bottom. The only useable water came from a small fire cart, a few buckets, and a small

Temporary Post Office after Fire

hook and ladder wagon. The fire was far too large to fight successfully, and within 2½ hours the entire business district had been burned. Virtually all retail stores were destroyed, and the contents of the Post Office was saved only by the frantic work of the postmaster, who ignored the pleas of his wife to come home and help protect their house from the raging fire.

Loss from this fire was estimated at $150,000. As most retailers were uninsured, many were faced with the total loss of their stores and their inventories. Although most of these buildings were crudely built wooden structures, assessed to be of little value and relatively easy to rebuild, it was the loss of their entire inventories that created severe hardship for many. In addition to the loss of Cambria's business district, six of the 50 homes near downtown were destroyed. Thankfully, no one died.

While some business owners left, many, including Lull, began rebuilding—some using brick— almost immediately. According to an article in the *San Luis Obispo Tribune* soon after the fire:

> *Mr. Leffingwell of Cambria made us a call yesterday, and we are glad to learn that disaster has only lent new life to the old pioneer town, and that in a very short time it will assume a condition of solidarity and finish that will place it far in advance of the old town.*

This prediction was initially correct, and soon many businessmen were busy rebuilding and restocking. For a while, the sound of construction echoed throughout the town and optimism grew as impressive new brick buildings began to replace the old wooden ones.

In addition to this burst of building activity, the Fire of 1889 forced residents to recognize their vulnerability in the face of neither firefighting capabilities nor water systems. Almost immediately, a volunteer fire department, with firefighting equipment, was established. Additionally, water issues were addressed as a result of this fire. First, better, more accessible water storage tanks were built. Also, spurred by the fire and with an eye to the future, J. D. Campbell, Jr. began studying Cambria's water problems. It took decades, but by 1913, he had privately developed the town's first water system, consisting of a good well and several storage cisterns. His plan to sell water to residents was hard to accomplish as all residents had their own wells. Nevertheless, his system was invaluable as Cambria grew.

Goodbye to Boom Times

Soon after the rebuilding from the devastating fire, citizens realized that the boom was over. The exciting days of staked claims and dreams of amazing lodes were gone, for mine production had petered out and mercury prices had fallen.

The parade of restless prospectors no longer flowed into Cambria, and almost overnight their raucous saloons had been replaced by social establishments more appropriate for solid, hard-working dairymen. The dangerous, exciting days of mineral wealth, bustling commercial seaports, and exciting horse races were replaced by a placid era as an isolated supply and service center to surrounding dairies.

Main Street, 1888

Dairying

Although the discovery of quicksilver temporarily generated excitement, headlines, and rapid growth, it was the steadily growing dairy ranches that provided Cambria's enduring economic foundation. Although this foundation spans Cambria's history from its earliest days, it was only after the first mining boom had ended that the centrality of dairying emerged.

Initially brought to stock mission land, huge herds of wild cattle roamed freely over the land surrounding Cambria during Spanish and Mexican years. The devastating drought of 1863-65 changed this. When virtually all cattle died, ranchers had some difficult decisions to make. Many gave up and selected another vocation; others focused on trying to rebuild herds. Most ranchers in Cambria decided to invest in good dairy/beef stock, rather than replacing the free-range cattle they had lost.

Their choice was a good one. Dairying thrived in the area around Cambria, and, by 1865, most ranchers had at least 20 dairy cows. Most also had hogs and were cultivating the land. Before long, dairies were producing more milk than could be consumed locally. As milk was too perishable to transport far, dairymen solved their transportation challenges by producing butter. Soon, steamers were regularly delivering butter from San Simeon to San Francisco. The magnitude of this trade was enormous. In the first six months of 1869, a mere five years since herds had been decimated, a single company shipped $30,000 worth of butter from San Simeon Bay to San Francisco. By 1873, 300,000 pounds of butter were being produced in the county annually. In less than a decade, Cambria ranchers had not only recovered completely from the devastating drought of 1863-65, but had established an industry that would serve as its economic foundation for the next century.

Many dairymen also raised hogs, for they thrived on the whey and skim milk left over when butter was produced. Eventually, hog production also outgrew local demand, and many were driven to Cayucos and San Simeon to be shipped to San Francisco. In one summer month as early as 1869, 2500 hogs were delivered to San Francisco. Shipping hogs created an interesting dilemma: How should one get these hogs on the ship? Some forced them to swim, even though hogs are not swimmers—and some always drowned. Others designed complicated apparatus to hoist them one-by-one onto the ship. As neither solution was very efficient, another solution—to cure them locally—resulted in a short-lived pork curing company that was established near Santa Rosa Creek. Although it produced high-quality bacon, lard, and sausages that were valued in San Francisco as well as locally, it failed after only two months due to lack of capital.

Although San Luis Obispo County led California in cheese making, producing 500,000 pounds in 1873 and increasing to 872,362 pounds by 1881, cheese making did not thrive in Cambria. In 1869, the first of what was to be a long succession of cheese factories was established at the future site of Harmony. By 1871, it had been sold twice but was beginning to prosper. During the best months of that year, when the grass was green, milk from 450 to 500 local cows produced 1200 pounds of cheese a day. Called the Excelsior Cheese Factory, it gained a reputation for quality. Cheese was sold wholesale for 17 to 18 cents per pound and, for a short time, competed well with the New York cheeses that were being imported.

In 1874, **Silas Williams** of Williams, Purdy, and Company purchased the Excelsior Cheese factory and instituted a profit-sharing cheese cooperative production model that had been very successful in New York. Members brought their milk to the cooperative where cheese was produced and shipped to market. Dairymen received the profit, less the 2.5% overhead that went to the Williams, Purdy, and Company. Despite the success of this model in New York, for some reason, it did not work as well for Cambria dairymen. By fall of that year, the Excelsior Cheese Factory had failed and closed.

The failure of these numerous attempts to establish a prosperous and stable cheese making industry in the Cambria area convinced dairymen that they would have to depend on flourishing milk, butter, and hog production for their economic stability. Before long, the dairymen began to unite and to work cooperatively. The first of these cooperatives, the Ranchers and Stock-raisers Cooperative Store, was organized in 1872, with the intent of cutting out the middlemen who had been profiting from the rapidly increasing dairy production. Owned by the dairymen, 2000 shares were offered at $20 each.

The rapid establishment of these dairies had a significantly positive impact on Cambria. Although many eyes in Cambria may have been focused on the exciting quicksilver discoveries, much of Cambria's growth resulted from its role as the supply and service center for the dairies. In addition to supplies, these dairymen needed skilled craftsmen and came to Cambria looking for them. Soon a wide array of craftsmen, including black- and tinsmiths, carpenters, wheelwrights, and cabinetmakers, were prospering there. Additionally, transport companies thrived and local laborers were fully employed. Well serviced by Cambria, these dairies, in turn, produced a wealth of dairy products and pork to feed the townspeople and, during boom years, hoards of hungry miners.

Pioneer Dairymen

Jeffrey Phelan, one of Cambria's earliest dairymen, settled two miles north of Cambria in 1857 before the town was established. Before long, Phelan, a well-respected citizen, was successfully raising stock, dairying, cultivating the land, and having children. Myron Angel wrote of him in his 1883 *History of San Luis Obispo County:*

> *People of the Anglo-Saxon race were exceedingly rare in that quarter, his eldest daughter being the first child born in that section of the county . . . . The dry seasons of 1862-1864 caused him very serious losses, but with his great energy and perseverance, he has been enabled to overcome them.*

Another early dairyman, **Morgan Brians**, was born in Kentucky in 1807 and moved to Missouri with his parents in 1817. He married and had six children in Missouri. In 1852, he and his six adult children endured a five-month trek across the plains to settle in California. They began dairying in Petaluma and stayed there until 1868, when they moved to Green Valley, between today's Cambria and Harmony. By 1883, they had the largest dairy ranch in the area, with 1335 acres and 165 cows devoted to the production of butter.

Born on a farm in Pennsylvania, **Ira Van Gorden** had traveled West in 1845 with his extended family and all of his possessions in 11 wagons. They journeyed with 500 other wagons, including the ill-fated Donners, and eventually settled in the Santa Clara Valley. During the next few years, he fought Mexico under General Fremont, opened a lumber business, mourned the death of his first wife, Rebecca, and mined for gold during the Gold Rush of 1849 before moving to Los Angeles to buy and ship grapes to San Francisco.

After marrying his second wife, **Mary**, and raising beef cattle for 11 years, they moved to the Cambria area and purchased the 4468 acres that had comprised Rancho San Simeon for $10,000. Within a year, they had sold 1500 acres to 5 speculators at prices estimated to be over $7 per acre. They raised beef and dairy cattle and hogs, grew hay, and planted extensive fruit orchards on the remaining land. Over the years, they sold other portions of their land and divided the rest between their six children and Ira's two sons from his first marriage. As early ranchers, the Van Gordens not only helped to establish Cambria's dairy industry, but, by dividing their land, also made it possible for many new Cambrians, both their descendants and newcomers, to participate in the establishment of this young town.

The first of a family that would help build the foundations of Cambria, **Peter Taylor**, a Scotsman, purchased 200 acres in Green Valley in 1869. Beginning as a grain rancher, he moved into dairying, where he prospered and continued to buy land until he owned 1100 acres replete with three sets of ranch buildings. His brothers, **John** and **James**, followed him here and soon began dairying and lumbering, also continuing to acquire property, until the Taylors owned several thousand acres of prime dairy, beef, and timber acreage.

Despite the rapid success of these early dairy ranchers, some were not successful. The ranch founded by **John Lehman**, and currently the home of Dawn Dunlap, Cambria's amazing historian, faced hard times. **Louisa Lehman's** recollections (told by her daughter) reveal the challenges faced by these dairying pioneers. She describes steep hills, unwelcoming neighbors, loneliness, and cows that were threatening and difficult to handle. She and her husband, John, suffering from a serious case of consumption, traveled on the newly completed railroad from Dayton, Ohio, heading to San Jose with three other families. En route, they met **Levi Blunt**, who convinced them of the wonderful opportunities awaiting them in San Luis Obispo County—and they changed their plans. They arrived in Cambria in 1869, and all three families settled on adjoining homesteads 7½ miles east of the town.

Coming from a flat, well-settled area in Ohio, Louisa struggled with her fears, ranging from the dizzying mountains and a forbidding terrain, to resentful Californios and uncooperative cows. Her daughter told of her fear of the mountains:

> *The mountains terrified my mother at first and she told me that when she first came, she would get on her hands and knees when she got to the top to look over the other side.*

Local Mexicans had been running cattle on this land for decades. When the settlers gained title to the land and began to cultivate it, they also built fences that made it impossible for the locals to continue using it. Naturally, they resented these newcomers. According to Louisa's daughter:

> *They would drive their stock onto my father's land and stand guard. When my father protested they would threaten his life. On one such occasion I was told my father bared his chest and told them to shoot – and so for many years it was the old story of line fences, rights-of-way and contested claims.*

Louisa also described cows that were initially not contented, calm, and well-behaved, but hard to manage and frightening. When John was away and she had to milk cows, she was so frightened that she donned his clothes and pulled his hat way down in hopes of fooling the cows into letting her milk them. This ruse must have worked, for Louisa was always able to complete the milking.

Five years after they arrived, John died. With five children to raise and a homestead to develop, according to her daughter, Louisa "although pitifully homesick and was burdened with overwhelming responsibility . . . took up life with almost unbelievable determination." Her family in Ohio begged her to return. Although she refused, her children remembered her crying each time a letter from her mother arrived. Eventually she did get to take her three youngest children to spend the summer with some family members in St. Joseph, Missouri. Unfortunately, Louisa and her family had to rush back to Cambria when the dairy herd sickened with Texas Tick Fever. Many died, and it took years for the ranch to flourish again, but it eventually recovered. Years later, her daughter recalled, "The sight even now of a flock of buzzards fills me with an ominous dread."

When Louisa died in 1898 while visiting her family, her adult children managed the ranch until they sold it in 1929. Through tenacity and endless hard work, Louisa, a widowed mother of five struggling to establish a ranch, survived. Many were not as lucky: Statistics reveal that more women suffered from insanity in isolated coastal areas, such as Cambria, than anywhere else in San Luis Obispo County.

These early Cambria dairy ranchers, such as the Phelans, Brians, Van Gordens, Taylors, and Lehmans, typified many of Cambria's earliest settlers, and laid the foundations upon which Cambria was established. Following these dairymen came the first of many Italian-speaking Swiss, who settled in Cambria and eventually emerged as the leading dairymen in the area.

Swiss-Italian Dairymen

During the middle of the 19th century, young men from Italian-speaking regions of Switzerland faced economic problems and gloomy futures. Word of California gold spread and, by 1852, many single, young Swiss men were leaving their jobs and heading for the California gold fields.

The trip was difficult, and more than 10% died en route. They arrived with little cash, no English, and minimal skills. Although few struck it rich in the gold fields, most obtained manual labor jobs on the Marin County ranches that were prospering by feeding hungry miners. Most came alone, but maintained close ties to their homeland and encouraged their countrymen to follow them to California. As word of plentiful work in California spread, more fol lowed. Although most were initially hired as milkers for minimal wages ($10 to $15 per month, plus food and lodging), it was not long until these Swiss immigrants managed many of the Marin County dairy ranches.

Swiss-American Parade, 1900

These young, stable, hard-working, and family-oriented men came in groups and remained together. Although they preferred to marry Swiss-Italian women, so few eligible women emigrated that many married outside their group or did not marry at all. Those who did marry had large families. Although they used their native dialect at home, they encouraged their children to learn English. Many of their children were given American names, and most of these children adapted well to California culture.

Many of these early immigrants missed their homeland terribly. A large number returned to Switzerland, but almost all of them were unable to re-adapt to the Old Country and eventually returned to California. Soon, despite their success in Marin County dairies, many wanted ranches of their own and sought inexpensive, available land suited to dairying. When they saw the lands surrounding Cambria, they knew that their dreams had come true.

Most came with visions, dairying skills, and energy—but little money. Many had to begin by working on one of Cambria's dairy ranches, often milking over 20 cows twice a day, plus a myriad of other ranching duties. It was a hard life that left many of them with "Swiss Diamonds," today widely known as carpel tunnel syndrome. Focused on eventually acquiring their own land, they lived conservatively and worked hard. Many were soon able to rent land and begin buying their own stock. The next step, purchasing land, was often very difficult, as land in the Cambria area was highly valued. Nevertheless, they continued to work hard and save, waiting for property to be offered for sale. When land did become available, they lent money to, and refused to bid against, one another. Slowly, more and more were successful in acquiring land. They continued saving their money—to help their countrymen buy their own land.

Before long, a number of families, including the **Barlogios**, **Bassis**, **Stornis**, **Bianchinis**, **Filipponis**, and the **Bassettis**, had settled in Cambria. These Swiss ranchers eventually became the backbone of its dairy industry. Among the earliest were the **Fiscalinis**. In 1876, **Joseph** journeyed from Switzerland to New York, took a train to San Francisco, a boat to San Simeon, and had walked the 15 miles from San Simeon to Green Valley. Fiscalini began milking for the large Morgan Brians Dairy, and within two years, was able to save enough money to form a partnership to lease land and 60 cows from George Hearst. He and his partner earned $1000 the first year, and Joseph immediately began buying cows of his own.

By 1885, he had accumulated enough money to begin acquiring land. Also in 1885, he married Margherita, his first cousin in San Francisco. Shortly after the wedding, he returned to Cambria alone to earn enough money to support her. Within a year, he had saved enough to send for her and begin a family. Before long, they had five children and the beginnings of a Cambria dynasty.

Soon after the children were born, Joe Fiscalini, like many other Swiss-Italian immigrants, realized he was homesick. He leased his ranch and took his family home to Switzerland. They stayed for eight years. Eventually, Joe and Margherita concluded that there was not enough in Switzerland for their sons. In hopes of keeping their family together, they returned to their Cambria dairy. They were successful. By adulthood, their children were running the business together and buying more and more ranches in the region. During this time, other Fiscalini family members from Switzerland had joined them. Prolific and prosperous, by 1960, there were 45 Fiscalinis living in the area.

These Swiss dairymen, in striking contrast to the rough miners congregating in Cambria, were sober, hard-working, and stable. They added a unique texture to the community and can be credited with establishing the solid foundation Cambria enjoys today. Although dairying in the Cambria area began decreasing in the 1930s due to increased government regulations, a large number of the descendents of these Swiss-Italian ranchers remain in the area today.

Portuguese Settlers

Before the refining of kerosene, oil rendered from whales lit lamps throughout the world. It wasn't long after ships from the East began to visit California's coast that the abundance of whales in the area was noted. Word traveled quickly and, before long, whalers had journeyed from a great distance to California to exploit these valuable mammals. Captain Joseph Clark came all the way from the Azores and opened a whaling station at San Simeon. Not unsurprisingly, others from Portugal followed and, before long, there was a growing population of men from Portugal working with Clark.

When oil was discovered in Pennsylvania in 1859, kerosene replaced whale oil and the industry declined. As it waned (the whaling station closed in 1894), the Portuguese began to seek other occupations. Many began to ranch, and either worked for Hearst or rented land from him. As they saved money, some were able to purchase their own land and to begin dairying and cultivating their own fields. In addition to being successful dairymen, this group is credited with introducing the lucrative cultivation of beans to the area. As most had large families, many of their descendents continue to live in Cambria today.

Prosperous Years

Within a few decades, the region had emerged as one of the state's most important dairying areas. According to a statement by the Board of Supervisors in November 1880:

> *As the county was proven the best for grazing in the State when cattle were grown for beef, hides, tallow, and horns alone, the same qualities render it, par excellence, the best dairying county of a more advanced period. San Luis Obispo was once in derision called the great "cow country" of California, and now it may boast of the title.*

By 1881, there were 50 dairy ranches in the Cambria area, each with an average of more than 70 cows. Records by dairyman and County Supervisor **J. C. McFerson** for May 1883 indicate a flourishing business:

Average product of each cow in butter	*$45*
Average worth of calf	*$10*
Average worth of hog fed on the milk	*$10*
Total products per cow	*$65*

In April of that year, weekly production of butter was as high as 1400 pounds a month, producing a total of 21,100 pounds of butter in 1881. By 1883, production had increased three-fold and resulted in 68,200 pounds of butter shipped from San Simeon that year. In addition to its impressive quantity, its quality was excellent. According to Myron Angel:

> *Cambria . . . butter commands the highest prices, or, as it is denominated, it is "gilt-edged" the retail price being from twenty-seven and one-half to forty cents per pound.*

Despite this impressive yield, butter production was difficult. Added to the hardships of caring for the cows and constantly milking was the tedious work of churning the butter by horsepower. Once the butter was ready, it had to be shipped by boat to San Francisco, via either Leffingwell or San Simeon Wharf or hauled to Cayucos or San Luis Obispo over rough roads, across often-raging creeks and around washed-out bridges. Early in the 20th century, changes had begun to make production less tedious. Centrifugal cream separators began to appear in the area and, before long, trucks were delivering milk and butter to San Luis Obispo on improved roads in the amazing time of only 8 hours roundtrip. In high production months, as many as 150 cans of cream and 10,000 to 12,000 pounds of butter were hauled per day.

By 1894, two more cooperative creameries were organized, the Home Creamery, adjacent to San Simeon Creek, and the Cambria Creamery. Both were reasonably successful for 10 years, but burned down within a month of one another. Dairymen were not distraught to see them burn, as they had begun to realize that they were not receiving optimal profit from them. They suspected that this was due to the poor management and unsanitary, inefficient operations that resulted in inferior butter.

Instead of forming another cooperative immediately, by 1912, there were four highly competitive creameries, three in Cambria and one in Harmony, that bought all that local dairymen could produce. During peak season, a single one of these creameries processed 2 tons of butter a day, molded it into pounds, cut it into cubes, wrapped it, and shipped it to San Francisco.

Cheese making, having failed repeatedly in Cambria, was finally successful under the leadership of **Marius George ("M.G.") Salmina**.

M. G. apprenticed as a blacksmith, but soon left that vocation to begin milking and learning about dairy processing. (He even took a dairy processing course at University of California, Berkeley.) When he came to live on his brother **Paul's** ranch in Harmony, they began experimenting by making cheese. Needing more room, they leased and refurbished some vacant buildings that had been built in 1869 and had been used by the short-lived Excelsior Cheese Factory co-op. By 1908, the Salminas began the Diamond Creamery and Cheese Factory.

Although small, the operation was successful, M. G. soon became convinced that the profit was in butter rather than cheese, and he began to focus much of his energy on making excellent butter. He learned that to make high-quality butter one needed the highest quality of cream. To achieve this, he initiated the policy of paying dairymen differing amounts dependent on the quality of the cream they brought. Initially opposed, when Diamond Butter's reputation for quality grew and profits followed, dairymen agreed that M. G. had been wise in his policies.

By 1911, M. G. was convinced this plant should become a cooperative. Throughout 1911 and 1912, he met with dairymen to try to convince them to join this co-op, despite their bad experiences with previous cooperatives. Needless to say, they were reluctant. After much convincing, they agreed, and, in 1913, 22 charter members formed the Harmony Valley Creamery Association. M. G. leased the plant and equipment to the co-op for $100 a month and was hired by them as its manager for $100 a month. Successful immediately, during the first year, the plant produced 238,000 pounds of butter and 110,000 pounds of cheese.

In 1918, M. G. sold the plant and equipment to the Association. By 1921, the Association had been invited to join the statewide marketing cooperative, Challenge Cream and Butter Association. After much discussion, members voted to join this large statewide group. By 1921, **Carl Hanson**, well known as an expert butter maker, was named chief cheese and butter maker as well as general superintendent for the Harmony plant. Electricity was installed in 1922, and by 1924, the plant was so busy that it needed to be expanded.

Business continued to boom, as witnessed by the 1.3 million pounds of butter produced in 1925.

By 1928, it was clear that the Association had grown so much that a more central location was needed, and San Luis Obispo was clearly the preference. After scrambling to raise the $42,000 necessary to buy land, finance a new building, and purchase modern equipment, the new plant opened in 1930. Despite being in the throes of the Great Depression, the Association prospered, and had soon recouped its initial investment. Much credit for this goes to M.G., who ran the plant with managerial genius. After the San Luis Obispo plant opened, the Harmony plant was used as a milk collection center, an Association-run garage to service members' trucks, and a small co-op store.

Although milk and cream production was their focus, these dairy ranches also cultivated the land and planted verdant orchards. Before long, the area had become one of the major agricultural centers in California with large orchards; crops of barley, wheat, and beans; and hogs. Twice as much flaxseed was produced in San Luis Obispo as in all other California counties combined and, when added to Santa Barbara County's yield, its bean production was the highest in the state. These were good years for dairymen, blessed with not only rich dairy ranches, but also some of California's finest agricultural land.

Regulatory Changes

In the first few decades of the 20th century, increasingly complex sanitation requirements and government regulations made it more and more difficult for the small dairymen of Cambria to prosper. By the 1920s, the Phelans, Cambria's pioneer diary ranchers, had stopped dairying and were raising beef cattle. Likewise, by the 1930s, the Fiscalinis were no longer dairying. They were the first in a continuing trend and, by the 1960s, most of the small diaries had disappeared. Some were unable to comply with expanding governmental requirements and remain profitable. Others were forced to sell out when they could not afford high inheritance taxes.

Although production stayed the same, membership in the Harmony Valley Creamery Association had dropped from a high of 400 in 1936 to only 53 in 1964.

Replacing these dairy ranches that had such a significant role in establishing the Cambria of today, are the beef cattle ranch, some irrigated agricultural land, and an alarming number of housing developments. Nevertheless, when one gazes over the lovely hills of Cambria, one can imagine the thriving small dairies that once dotted the landscape.

Decades of Isolation, 1894-1920

Soon after the Fire of 1889, many began to realize that Cambria's boom years were over. During the 1870s and 1880s, Cambria, with its well-producing quicksilver mines and prosperous, rapidly growing dairy farms, appeared to be on the road to a vibrant future. Residents couldn't envision the decreased quicksilver production, the looming changes at San Simeon, or the negative impact of the San Luis Obispo railroad.

With hindsight, most experts agree that 1880 was Cambria's peak of prosperity and growth. Following that good year were 15 relatively good years, marred only by slowly diminishing profits and growth. By the mid-1890s, this trend culminated in widespread stagnation. The promise of the1880s was never realized and, instead, ushered in nearly four decades of minimal growth and increasing isolation.

Changes at San Simeon

When George Hearst died in 1891, he left his San Simeon holdings, in addition to a $20 million fortune, to his wife, **Phoebe**. His San Simeon empire was comprised of the large Hearst Ranch and wharf, plus a number of small rental farms. By the late 1890s, Phoebe and her family adopted a new policy: They began increasing the rental rates on these small farms.

Although rents may have been increased in order to net more income, the result was just the opposite. Rental rates were increased so much that most tenants were forced to leave. Dairy farmers were the first to feel the economic hardship. The more resourceful ones used their savings and borrowed from friends and family to purchase their own land. Thankfully, land did occasionally become available for those who could afford to purchase, and some were able to acquire their own land. For example, the *San Luis Obispo Tribune* carried the following notice in July 1897:

$3000, 474 acres with six fine springs, also one cold sulpher spring, 6 acres of orchard all bearing trees, small dairy building. The piece is fenced and is located on San Simeon Creek about 8 miles from Cambria.

Unfortunately, the less affluent were forced off the land and left to find work in San Luis Obispo or another promising town.

When the renters left, the local merchants of San Simeon suffered and, after 1910, only one store remained. The sharp reduction in production in the San Simeon area also severely reduced shipping from the San Simeon Wharf, and optimistic dreams of a vibrant commercial seaport at San Simeon faded. Additionally, Cambria businesses suffered.

The Railroad

More significant than San Simeon's decline was the completion of the railroad to San Luis Obispo in 1894. Almost immediately, the preferred mode of transportation shifted from coastal shipping to rail. Although the demise of coastal shipping was a foregone conclusion, Cambrians persisted in their efforts to build a pier to address their transportation needs. In 1908, the Cambria County Wharf, at the mouth of Santa Rosa Creek, was almost complete when a storm demolished it. The loss, totaling $21,240, was borne by the county.

After the railroad began to serve San Luis Obispo, steamers came to San Simeon less and less frequently until 1915 when regular steamer service ceased. In 1916, the last ship to use the Port of San Simeon left, never to return. Cambria, established as a commercial crossroads between San Luis Obispo and San Simeon, was in a perfect location as long as shipping and commerce at San Simeon thrived. When San Simeon declined, Cambria's coastal location was no longer a benefit, but, instead, an impediment to prosperity.

As San Luis Obispo emerged as a self-sufficient transportation center, Cambria was forced to depend on it for all its transportation needs. Unfortunately, access to San Luis Obispo was still difficult.

Roads remained unimproved, and the trip continued to take 8 to 14 hours of tedious travel. While Cambria's isolation increased, inland towns grew as roads were built to connect them. Soon, Cambria had lost its place as second largest town in the county to other inland towns served by these improved roads. Within months of the arrival of the railroad to San Luis Obispo, Cambria had transitioned from a vibrant crossroads to a forgotten outpost, a quiet farming community dependent on poorly maintained, inadequate roads.

A Small, Cohesive Community

Cambria settled into its placid role as the quiet supply center serving the surrounding dairies. This period, while quiet, witnessed its change from a transportation nexus into an isolated, tightly-knit community, with a unique character and common experience.

Much of this cohesiveness sprang from fraternal organizations, for a large majority of Cambrians belonged to at least one of these organizations. The Masons came early and were well-established by 1869. Within a decade, most national organizations had established a branch in Cambria. In addition to the better known orders, Cambria was the home to some unique societies, including the American Legion of Honor, which weathered controversy by allowing women to join; the Order of Missourians; and the Order of Chosen Friends, a life insurance group that believed in fun and good times.

In addition to its fraternal organizations, it was during these years that Cambria became famous for its community celebrations. Wondrous picnics were held on the Fourth of July, May Day, Swiss Independence Day and almost any other day locals wanted to celebrate. And what grand picnics they were–replete with parades, flags draped everywhere, barbecues, colorful costumes from Swiss ranchers, music, speeches, skits, and, soon, baseball. Baseball became so popular that, before long, the town had its own team, the Cambria Kelp Eaters, a squad that quickly earned a good reputation throughout the county. Favorite dates, such as Fourth of July and California Admission Day (September 9), drew as many as 2000 to celebrate and accentuated Cambria's reputation for hosting wonderful festivities.

During these stagnant years, the lives of Cambria's citizens were anything but placid. And, typical of small towns, stories of personal dramas were shared throughout the town. Everyone was talking about the shocking death of the town's physician, **Dr. Freeman**, who had delivered most of the town's babies, when a love triangle resulted in his shooting by a jealous **Rocha Daniels**. They also got involved when **George Allen** murdered **Tony Mariano** in a disagreement over a fence line. Mariano was the son of Joseph and Maria, Portuguese whalers-turned-saloon keepers who ran Mariano's Saloon, at the site of today's Camozzi Saloon, Cambria's

Tony Mariano, behind the Bar, in his Saloon

last "cowboy" bar. According to reports, Allen insulted Mariano who then slapped him. They parted angry, and later that afternoon, Allen returned with a gun and shot Mariano. He bled to death where he fell, while Allen escaped on a fast horse. When he was captured and tried, the testimony of a witness who recounted Mariano's slap saved him from conviction. The consensus of the jury was that the slap rendered Mariano as the initial aggressor. Though many agreed that murder was an overreaction to a slap, Allen was never punished.

Saloons continued to be busy, and tales of drunken behavior provided almost daily conversation for locals. According to a June 1896 article in the *San Luis Obispo Tribune*:

> *Tramps are again plentiful. In some cases they seem to be poor unfortunate creatures to whom the world owes a living and deals it out stiltedly, while in others they seem a tough and indolent set.*

By 1917, continuing rowdiness had so frustrated citizens that Cambria's third jail was built. It was constructed with heavy planks and double-barred doors to withstand an attack from inside or out. It was so tightly constructed that, soon after it was completed, a young man set his mattress on fire by accident and nearly suffocated from the smoke. So shocked were citizens that the jail was never used again.

Schooling was important to the young town, spurring establishment of its first high school. There was a great deal of pride in the accomplishments of its graduates. The class of 1895 consisted of four, three of whom went to Stanford, while the fourth selected Berkeley. According to an editorial in the *San Luis Obispo Tribune*, "We are proud of our young teachers and schools. Though but a one horse town, we'll get there just the same."

Cambria's Newspapers

Although local tales were commonly shared quickly, via an unofficial grapevine, Cambria depended on the *San Luis Obispo Tribune* for its county, state, national, and local news. Nevertheless, citizens wanted their own newspaper and were thrilled to read in the April 9, 1915 *San Luis Obispo Tribune* that the *Cambria Courier*, Cambria's third try at establishing a newspaper, was about to begin publication. The *San Luis Obispo Tribune* reported that **C. B. Langley** was coming to Cambria, bringing his printing equipment with him. The first issue was expected before May 1915. Citizens waited and waited. Finally a full year later, in June 1916, the *Cambria Courier* began publication.

By this time, C. B. Langley was gone, and 27 year old **Clyde A. Meacham** had purchased the equipment. When he arrived, he found that he had purchased a shop in total disarray. Undaunted, he settled into his portion of 4111 Bridge Street, the rest of which was a blacksmith shop. (This location would later become a saloon, known as "The Bucket of Blood" for fights there on Saturday nights.) Only after months of unscrambling type was he able to begin to publish. Despite all Meacham's good work to bring order to the print shop, the *Cambria Courier* was out of business a mere 1½ years later. By January 4, 1918, the third of Cambria's newspapers had died an early death, and citizens had to wait another 13 long years for a newspaper that would survive.

During these years, Cambria was a closely woven community with a largely provincial focus. Symbolic of this provincialism was the newsworthiness of the 1916 regulation that prohibited herding cattle through downtown Cambria and residential neighborhoods. Despite this isolation, there were signs that a new era of vibrancy was just around the corner. Although it took the arrival of the automobile to give Cambria the centrality it desired, the influx of Asian immigrants and the impact of World War I were early signs that Cambria was about to shed its isolation.

Chinese Come to Cambria

Many of Cambria's earliest Chinese had come to America to labor on the railroads that were crisscrossing the nation. When local work was complete, many followed the railroad as it connected other cities. Others went to work for **Ah Louis**, the successful San Luis Obispo entrepreneur, who prospered by hiring and managing his countrymen at work throughout the county. When quicksilver mines were prospering, Ah Louis brought his laborers to Cambria. When this work was done, most returned to their community in San Luis Obispo to await the next job.

Others who did work for Ah Louis began squatting in simple shacks along the coast between Monterey and Cambria. Initially working as abalone fishermen, most of these squatters eventually cultivated the prolific sea lettuce that thrived along the rocky coast. At low tide, they clambered over the treacherous rocks, harvesting this sea lettuce. Soon, many were giving nature a boost: They identified the rocks on which the sea lettuce thrived, and scrubbed, scorched, and burned all other algae off them. With no competition, the sea lettuce soon grew prolifically on these selected rocks.

Sea lettuce was delivered to San Francisco in 300-pound bales and was then shipped to Hong Kong. There, it was used to manufacture precious Chinese medicine. Initially transported by sea from San Simeon, records show that, as early as 1869, $3000 worth of sea lettuce was shipped. By 1880, 104 bales were shipped. After 1894, it was transported to San Francisco by rail from San Luis Obispo.

Some also dried abalone to add to their income until a law, just after the turn of the 20th century, declared the selling of dried abalone to be illegal. Denied this lucrative source of income, some seaweed farmers continued to risk legal repercussions by hiding dried abalone in their bales of seaweed to bring some needed extra income. Eventually, seaweed farmers along Cambria's coast left, abandoning their simple shacks that had dotted the coastal landscape.

For a short time early in the 20th century, Cambria hosted a vibrant Chinese community center. This center was built on a lot at 2264 Center Street that had been owned by George Rothschild, the merchant who had shocked the town by committing suicide in 1873. Abram Gans, Rothschild's former partner, acquired this lot. While the Gans family owned it, they allowed the Chinese to build two laundries, several small residences, and a social hall that housed an altar, a meeting area, and bunks in which one could smoke opium. Although few lived there full-time, this center provided a welcome place for Chinese vacationers and young bachelors to socialize, relax, worship, and gamble.

Although locals whispered tales of opium abuse, overindulgence in rice wine, excessive gambling, and murders, little evidence of these activities exists. There is much evidence, though, of grand celebrations each Chinese New Year, when the entire Chinese coastal population gathered in Cambria to indulge in roast pig, rice wine, and gambling, while enjoying an impressive fireworks display.

By 1916, most Chinese had left Cambria for San Francisco, and their buildings had been either sold or fell into disrepair. In 1918, the Warren family purchased the Center Street lot and tore down many of the dilapidated structures that had comprised the Chinese community center. They combined the altar room of the social hall and a building that had been used as Cambria's first high school to create their home. Amazingly, this altar room, estimated to have been built in 1889, shortly after the Fire, has survived and is one of the only remaining altar rooms in California. Today, it totters—jacked up from its foundation—dilapidated and abandoned, awaiting the next phase of its interesting history.

Whisper of Prosperity

Soon after the beginning of the 20th century, mercury prices were on the rise yet again, and promising mining operations were beginning to produce. Elmer Scott Rigdon, son of one of Cambria's founding families, persuasive orator, bank owner, and the politician who convinced the state to build the Big Sur Highway, found himself temporarily in charge of a quicksilver mine. Here's how it happened:

Just after the turn of the century, **H. J. Price** and **Henry W. Martin** found cinnabar on some foreclosed property 8 miles northeast of Cambria that pioneer dairyman, Jeffrey Phelan, had purchased for $5 an acre from the Cambria Bank. Neither Price nor Martin knew that Phelan had not purchased the mineral rights of this land; Elmer Rigdon, president of the bank, had retained these rights. Martin excitedly told his friend, Rigdon, about the find. By 1903, Rigdon had staked his claim and started mining this land, leaving Price and Martin with nothing. Rigdon operated this mine, known as Bank Mine, until 1906, when it was sold and renamed Cambria Quicksilver Mine Company.

World War I (1914-1918)

Although the revitalization of mercury mining enriched Cambria before and during much of World War I, mercury was not the only resource that brought prosperity to Cambria during these years. During World War I, the abalone industry thrived and enjoyed good production and high prices. The industry was so good that, in 1917, an abalone processing plant was opened in Cambria. It prospered and processed as much as 150 pounds of abalone a day during the war. After World War I, prices fell, and the Cambria plant was relocated to Morro Bay.

For awhile, it appeared that Cambria would also benefit from the war-generated rise in the price of lumber. Unfortunately, when the local lumber industry went into full-scale production, owners were disappointed to discover that the second-growth timber in the area yielded a much poorer quality than the virgin lumber they had produced earlier. Mill operations were reduced significantly but never closed completely. Instead, they milled far lower quality wood that was used to produce cheap building materials. Gone forever was the high-quality lumber that had distinguished Cambria a mere half-century earlier.

During these war years, Cambria also welcomed two of its favorite residents. **Joaquin ("Jack") Soto** traveled to San Simeon in 1910 at the age of 14 to work on the Hearst Ranch. By 1914, he had left the Ranch and had settled in Cambria to work with his brother-in-law, who owned a half interest in a meat market on Bridge Street. By 1917, Jack had purchased this market and expanded it to carry a complete line of groceries. According to local legend, William Randolph Hearst strode into Soto's one day and bought all the meat and groceries, forcing Soto to close for a few days to restock. Still serving Cambria locals and visitors alike, Soto's Market was built at its current location in 1939, where Jack and his wife, Agnes, continued to work until he was well into his 80s.

For years, Cambria's two major grocery stores, Soto's Market and the Lyons' Red and White, maintained a friendly rivalry. When the

Red and White was sold by William Lyons, the owner's son, **Wilfred**, went to work full-time at Soto's Market, 6 days a week (in addition to stocking shelves on Sundays after church) and stayed for 43 years. Lyons, known throughout the town as "Mr. History," still lives in the center of downtown where he was born, and is an incredible resource to all who seek to learn the stories of this wonderful town.

Cambrians threw themselves into the war effort with enthusiasm and hard work. Almost immediately, a Red Cross chapter was formed. Volunteers in homes throughout Cambria began knitting socks, rolling bandages, and collecting donations for war-torn nations. They also waited anxiously for news of their loved ones. Many of the precious letters sent from battle were published in the young, short-lived *Cambria Courier*, and have become a valued record of those difficult days.

As the war was drawing to a close, the 1919 flu epidemic that swept Europe and the rest of the country hit Cambria hard. Many locals died from that horrible sickness, including Phoebe Hearst, wife of George and mother of William Randolph. On top of this tragedy, prices fell as soon as the war ended. Many of the mines and small industries that had opened and prospered throughout the war closed. Cambria was quiet again, and many expected it would resume its role as a quiet farm village.

They had not counted on the enormous changes just around the corner. As Detroit began producing more and more of those amazing new horseless carriages, the end of Cambria's isolation loomed. It was when automobiles began to dot the California landscape after World War I, that Cambria's prospects began to brighten.

When that happened, changes began to transform Cambria. Car dealerships, garages, and gas pumps sprang up. Cambrians embraced the wondrous automobile and leapt joyfully into the post-World War I years, characterized by land developers and rising real estate prices. They also enthusiastically welcomed the vanguard of an exciting new breed of tourist: the motorist. Cambria celebrated its picturesque location and set about selling itself to all who could pay.

Roads, Developers, War, and a Castle, 1920-1964

Although much of Cambria's history centers on its unceasing battle against isolation, most agree that, without this isolation, it would not be the charming, peaceful town that is so appealing to so many today. Despite the charm of this isolation, Cambrians cheered the changes that decreased this isolation. During the years after World War I, they had many changes to cheer. Soon after the war, the automobile and improved roads began the transformation of Cambria. Even more significantly, these years witnessed the building of Hearst Castle, introducing an amazing group of people to Cambria, ranging from workers and artisans, to Hollywood stars.

Suddenly, Cambria was no longer off the beaten path, but was the perfect destination for America's newest tourist, the motorist. Midway between San Francisco and Los Angeles, Cambria was in the optimal location to welcome these new, mobile travelers. They needed a convenient place to stay and wanted the most modern accommodations. And, although the flood of tourists did not begin until after World War II, these vanguards found just what they needed when the home George Lull built for his bride was expanded and converted into Cambria's first tourist court, the Bluebird. Still offering warm, old-fashioned hospitality to visitors, the Bluebird symbolizes Cambria's joyous leap into the age of the automobile.

Once the first of these motorists began arriving, plans for an amazing road took shape. This ambitious new road had a powerful advocate: Elmer Rigdon, successful businessman and son of one of the town's founding fathers, was known throughout Cambria as a man who loved to talk. Ever since he was a young man, his speeches had impressed and entertained locals. Eventually he found the perfect outlet for his passion for speechmaking: politics. In 1917, he introduced a bill in the California Legislature that would forever change the Central Coast. He proposed a highway along the coast, linking San Simeon with Carmel.

He was persuasive and tenacious and, by 1924, construction of this huge highway project had begun. Three years and many contractors later, only 25 miles had been completed – the 12 from Piedras Blancas south to Salmon Creek and the 13 miles north from Big Sur to Anderson Canyon. Funds had run out and the project was at a standstill.

Years later, construction began again, using hundreds of convicts from San Quentin Prison encamped at each end and dynamiting their way through mountainsides towards each other. Trainload after trainload of explosives was used to blast away the rocks along the coast. Routinely, men were lowered over the side of the cliff to bore holes for enormous charges of dynamite. Finally, in 1937, at a cost of nearly $10 million and several lives, the road was completed. With one huge blast of dynamite, tons of rock fell into the ocean, the two convict camps were united, and Big Sur Highway 1 was complete.

Hearst Builds His Castle

After George Hearst's death, his widow, Phoebe, carried on his attempt to acquire adjacent land. She was successful and, by 1919, the Hearsts owned more than 14 miles of coastline and approximately 60,000 acres. By continuing to purchase land throughout the 1920s, their holdings grew to 250,000 acres. Although the Hearsts, especially William Randolph, did a wonderful job preserving native plants and wildlife on the vast estate, historic buildings were not as fortunate and these years saw the loss of important sites. Early San Simeon homesteads were left to ruin and the seaweed farmers' modest quarters were bulldozed so that transients would not use them.

Although William Randolph Hearst had become world-famous as the rich and controversial publisher of numerous newspapers, he continued to flee to San Simeon, where he found a unique and replenishing peace. Whenever possible, he would return to his favorite spot, a rough family campsite at the top of the hill. Years later, in 1930, he wrote lovingly of his refuge:

William Randolph Hearst

> *Now I am going to board a train and go down to my ranch and find my little hideaway on my hilltop at San Simeon, and look down on the blue sea, and up at the blue sky, and bask in the glorious sunshine of the greatest State of the greatest nation in the whole world.*

When his mother, Phoebe, died of the flu in 1919 and left the entire Hearst fortune to him, William Randolph knew it was time to build something more permanent at his favorite spot. His "little hideaway," initially planned as a bungalow, grew into the enormous country home we know today as Hearst Castle. Named "La Cuesta Encantada" (the Enchanted Hill), many believe it is the perfect example of Hearst's drive to do everything on a grand scale. Although it was never completed, the majority of the construction spanned almost three decades, from 1919 until 1947. Consisting of four Mediterranean-style buildings, containing 165 rooms and surrounded by two awesome swimming pools, acres of gardens, and hundreds of animals, from elephants and yaks to gazelles and polar bears, it was, according to Jespersen's *History of San Luis Obispo:*

an enormous mansion, medieval in style, . . . the art treasures of Europe were ransacked to furnish the "castle," and little San Simeon, so lately a whaling station, had the rather overwhelming experience of being the unloading port for museum pieces famous in history and valued at many thousands of dollars!

For years, despite its enormity and opulence, it was a private home, viewed with awe by tourists through the coin-fed telescope at San Simeon, five miles away. The powerful personality of William Randolph Hearst, the parade of world-famous treasures housed there, plus its inaccessibility, only served to add to its mystical and magical air.

During these years, Cambria benefited greatly from the creation of this Castle. Spanning the high unemployment years of the Great Depression, a large number of Cambria citizens found welcome employment there. Additionally, huge numbers of people came to build the Castle and serve its glittering guests. Many of them looked to Cambria for supplies and services, creating prosperity in Cambria in an unprosperous decade. Some of those who came, stayed. Some who stayed were artisans from the European guilds, who had come with their entire families to work on the Castle. Others who stayed were the staff of the Hollywood stars and the world's millionaires, who accompanied their bosses to the Castle and fell in love with Cambria.

These Castle-building years were good years in Cambria. In addition to providing Cambrians with a constant source of discussion, the construction years also provided them with both a welcome source of employment and extra income for their businesses. William Randolph, known in businesses circles as one of the world's most powerful, controversial, and demanding millionaires, came to the area on holiday and brought benefits to Cambria that have not been forgotten.

Enter the Developers

By the late 1920s, the land developers began to arrive. The **Jones Brothers, Harry, Robert** and **Clarence**, came from Hollywood and bought some of the rolling, pine-covered land surrounding the downtown area. Almost immediately, they established the Cambria Pines Development Company and began to survey, subdivide, and market their property. Before long, they had subdivided their land into 12,000 tiny 25-foot lots and had begun to market Cambria to the world. Rather than trying to sell their small lots as permanent residences, they marketed their subdivision as a recreational retreat, where folks could come on holiday and escape from their jobs and worries. They mounted a multi-pronged radio and print advertising campaign that lauded Cambria as a "fog-free" environment. Initially, they were very successful, and many purchased lots sight unseen.

Developers expected affluent professionals to buy. Unfortunately, few of the rich and famous purchased these tiny lots. One who did buy became one of Cambria's most colorful and controversial characters. In 1928, **Art Beal**, a trash collector and day laborer, purchased a steeply sloping lot on Hillcrest Drive and began a construction project lasting 51 years, using the most wondrous combination of scavenged materials. While some Cambrians watched in amusement, others were horrified. Using shells, beer cans, car parts, toilet fixtures and innumerable other pieces of junk, Beal built Cambria's most unusual house, "Nitwit Ridge." Listed as a California Historic Landmark, current owners offer guided tours of this amazing monument to the creative and unconventional spirit of its builder.

Although some did buy the Jones Brothers' lots, the Cambria Pines Development Company was the victim of bad timing. Almost as soon as their advertising began to get results and optimists foresaw a buying frenzy, the Stock Market Crash of 1929 changed everything. Suddenly, few had any discretionary funds to buy distant property on a whim, and sales diminished to almost nothing. Many who had signed a contract, never paid a penny. Those who had made a down payment, forfeited it. Before long, lots were selling for less than $100, and the Cambria Pines Development Company was in serious trouble. Despite their financial woes, it was during these years that the

Cambria Pines Development Company established an important Cambria institution. Shortly before the Crash of 1929, they built a rustic lodge and converted it into their headquarters. Used for lodging and social activities for prospective buyers, it was designed to make them so happy and comfortable that they would fall in love with Cambria and eagerly buy land. To accomplish this, it was expanded to include a clubroom for dancing and gambling and, amazingly, a complete zoo stocked with doves, alligators, monkeys, peacocks, and 200 pheasants.

Although it accommodated prospective buyers as planned, it also became Cambria's social center and the site of innumerable celebrations and gatherings. Unexpectedly, during the Depression, it also became a popular and fashionable place for the affluent to escape from their worries. Capitalizing on this unexpected source of income, by 1932, it had been expanded to include 31 log cabins that were rented for $1.50 per night, $2 if one wanted electricity.

It is logical to surmise that the Lodge's prestige as an "in" place to stay and be seen would help land sales. Most expected that these affluent visitors would come to play and would stay to buy land on which to build their own retreats. After all, this had happened in Santa Barbara and other coastal towns only a few decades earlier. Unfortunately, this did not happen. Despite the popularity of the Lodge, lot sales continued to lag. It seems that those who could afford to stay at the Lodge were not interested in building homes in Cambria. Instead, they continued to party at the Lodge, while buying vacation homes elsewhere. Continuing this long tradition as a social center, the Cambria Pines Lodge still delights visitors with its rustic sophistication, stunning setting, and peaceful charm.

Although the Cambria Pines Development Company's land sales lagged, by 1930, it had formally filed the subdivision maps that were to define the shape of an important portion of Cambria's current residential community. Following a tradition of land speculation that has marked Cambria's entire history, this company was one of many that were soon to comprise one of Cambria's biggest industries: development and real estate. Today, more than 80 real estate agents and brokers continue the long-standing tradition of selling Cambria.

It was not until the 1950s, when much of coastal California experienced the post-World War II flood of new residents, that Cambria was rediscovered. With this population explosion, a new generation of buyers began to seek quiet, beautiful recreational areas. Soon, summer homes sprang up, and Cambria experienced a seasonal boom and prosperity. This trend accelerated when, in 1958, the state opened the William Randolph Hearst home as a State Historical Park. And, the tourists and summer residents have been coming to Cambria ever since.

Depression Years

During the years just before the Stock Market Crash of 1929, life in Cambria was quiet, but the future looked bright. The promise of prosperity hummed throughout the town. The automobile had reconnected Cambria to the rest of the world, land was subdivided and ready for the right purchasers, and an exceedingly interesting parade of affluent visitors were flocking to the Castle, with plenty of money to spend in Cambria.

While waiting for the expected land boom to begin, Cambria citizens cheered the arrival of electricity in 1927. They also enjoyed a good movie each Saturday night, for the arrival of the automobile age had also brought the traveling movie man, **Dick Gerdes**, to this once-isolated town. Beginning in the 1920s with silent movies, he traveled from town to town throughout Santa Barbara and San Luis Obispo counties with the movie of the week. He loved to fish for trout at Santa Rosa Creek, so he made sure that he stayed in Cambria long enough to get his fill of fishing each week. He arrived in Cambria on Friday night and showed his films, usually a serial, a main feature (often a cowboy Western), and a comedy each Saturday night. After the movies, all the benches were pushed to the sides of the room and the dancing began.

Just after the Crash, Cambria got yet another newspaper, the *Cambria News*. Unfortunately, this paper fared no better than Cambria's other failed newspapers and closed after only one year. Despite all these failures, the Depression years did finally bring Cambrians a paper that would last. In 1931, **Marcus Waltz** began publishing *The Cambrian*, the newspaper that is still providing citizens with their news. Finally, after enduring years of publishers who ranged from itinerant journalists to local boosters, Cambria had a professional publisher who was there to stay.

Despite the prosperity brought by the construction of Hearst Castle, the Great Depression did bring hard times to some by temporarily crippling tourism, real estate promotion, and abalone processing. Additionally, these years saw the beginning of the slow decline of the dairy industry. Unlike Santa Barbara and Newport Beach, which received a large amount of welcome funding from President Franklin D. Roosevelt's New Deal, Cambria received no windfall of federal funding. Instead, Cambrians continued to work hard, supply the Hearsts whenever possible, and wait for the better times just around the corner.

World War II

The December 7, 1941 attack on Pearl Harbor brought a disturbing, but very distant, European war to the shores of Cambria. Citizens went from feeling isolated and insulated to keeping constant vigilance and preparing for a coastal attack. This war hit home quickly when, by the end of December 1941, the tanker ***S.S. Montebello*** was attacked and sunk off Cambria. Immediately, Cambrians threw themselves into the war effort. They welcomed the Army Corps of Engineers, who leased Cambria Pines Lodge from 1942 until end of the war, and focused a great deal of attention to guarding their coastline from enemy attack.

Before Pearl Harbor, life went on as usual for most, memorable for such simple pleasures as the two-night run of the popular movie, *One Night in Lisbon*, starring Fred MacMurray, for 39 cents (adults) and 17 cents (children). Many Cambrians hoped that war could be avoided. Some were such staunch isolationists that Patrick O'Brien blasted them in *The Cambrian* of November 27, 1941, by saying:

> *If, as they tell us, Great Britain is practically dead, of what use would our isolation be to us if the world was ruled by Hitlerism or Communism?*

All this changed when the attack brought the United States into the war and gave Cambrians a real reason to watch their shores for enemy attack. Cambrians knew that attack could come at anytime, and they mobilized to defend the nation by constant vigilance. Before long, volunteer women had been assigned to watch for Japanese planes from 6 a.m. until 9 p.m., seven days a week. They observed for three hours. This coverage required five women each day, 35 per week. Additionally, 23 substitutes were scheduled to fill in when needed. They were trained to report to the chief local observer, who relayed any concerns to headquarters in Riverside. Additionally, the Coast Guard continually conducted beach patrols.

Although never intercepting an attack, they could have. Intelligence information captured after the war confirmed that the Japanese had planned to shell all major coastal communities on Christmas Day 1941. Luckily, the United States' vigorous anti-submarine maneuvers following Pearl Harbor forced the Japanese submarines to retreat and the Japanese command to cancel its December 25 attack. Had this not happened, Cambria could have been one of the coastal communities shelled on Christmas Day 1941.

Although the Japanese did not shell coastal towns, shortly after Pearl Harbor, 12 of Japan's most modern and lethal 300-foot submarines lurked a short distance off the West Coast. Their mission was to sink the three United States Navy aircraft carriers, ***Lexington, Saratoga,*** and ***Enterprise***, which had escaped destruction at Pearl Harbor by being at sea. They were especially interested in the ***Lexington***, for reports indicated that it was heading toward the West Coast. The Japanese deployed their new, heavily armed submarines to patrol an area stretching from the Straits of Juan de Fuca in northern Washington State to San Diego, with orders to sink the ***Lexington***.

Although the Japanese did not sink the ***Lexington*** until the Battle of the Coral Sea, they did a great deal of damage to other ships in their path. During these early days of the war, they sank seven American ships along the West Coast, in addition to a pair of unescorted Russian submarines sailing along the coast. The largest of these sank so quickly that all aboard died, a serious military blunder, as Japan was not then at war with Russia.

This Japanese submarine activity shook up Cambrians when, at 6 a.m. on December 23, 1941, the Japanese submarine, I-21, torpedoed and sank the 8000-ton Union Oil tanker, ***S.S. Montebello***. Running empty, the tanker had left Port San Luis at 2 a.m. that day with its captain and 35 crewmen. The explosion of the torpedo woke the town. When it was hit, the ***S.S. Montebello*** was six miles south of Piedras Blancas. It sank a mere 45 minutes after it was hit.

Before it went down, four lifeboats, holding all 36 men, had been deployed. The Japanese submarine surfaced briefly and its crew fired 14 shots from its deck gun at the ***S.S. Montebello's*** crew as they were getting into the lifeboats. None was injured in this Japanese assault. Three of the lifeboats, holding 30 of the men, drifted safely to Cayucos. The fourth lifeboat and its six occupants was soon sighted drifting toward the rough surf offshore Cambria. Cambrians rallied and, before long, 21 were helping with the rescue. One, **J. Neil Moses**, the editor of the *Morro Bay Sun*, recalled his observations in the January 1, 1942 issue of *The Cambrian*:

> *Four men were seen straining at the oars. Another was bailing water. A sixth man, obviously the skipper of the torpedoed tanker Montebello, was sitting tensely at the stern of the lifeboat using an oar for a tiller.*

The sea was a tempest, and the wind was blowing a gale. On they came, slowly, laboriously. They were heading for the rocks, but they couldn't help it. With each mountainous swell it looked like the storm-tossed lifeboat would capsize. . . .

On they came, inching closer and closer to exposed and partially submerged rocks. They were straining with every ounce of energy they possessed, but it looked like they were doomed to crack up on a jagged 20 feet of the outcropping. The skipper, for some reasons unexplained, plunged into the sea and made it to the rock just as a big swell struck him. He was unable to grasp anything and the back-sweep of the swell carried him 30 yards out.

A husky young man, who turned out to be David Chase of Morro Bay, had stripped and plunged into the sea to take a line to the skipper who was held afloat by his lifebelt. The skipper was too exhausted to struggle and was just drifting in the swells. By using an oar, Chase finally made contact and the two were towed in.

Finally the lifeboat crashed into the shore rock. . . . There was a wild scramble by four of the men. One or two made it after a drenching. Two others floundered in the sea, but managed to get a hand on to the lines. . . . In the meantime, the sixth man, Fireman Edgar F. Smith, perhaps the wisest of the lot, had stayed with the boat. It drifted around the outjutting rock and into a very small cove. A swell lifted its bow momentarily into a rock and Smith climbed on it and there remained out of reach of the water until he had rested.

While some stood in the frigid, turbulent surf rescuing crewmen, others administered first aid and poured hot coffee for them. Although crewmen and rescuers alike were injured and chilled by the rocky landing, no lives were lost. Soon, all six crewmen had been dried, warmed, treated, fed and taken by ambulance (driven by a young Japanese-American soldier) to rejoin their shipmates. Their bravery and quick thinking were lauded by their captain, **Olaf Eckstrom**, when he was interviewed shortly after the rescue: "God bless 'em–they performed like American seamen, orderly, efficiently, without hysteria."

Waltz, editor of *The Cambrian,* was another of the rescuers. As a writer for the *San Francisco Call-Bulletin,* he made sure that this major newspaper covered the story. As it turns out, it was the only major paper to cover the sinking of the ***S.S. Montebello,*** as Secretary of the Navy Frank Knox did everything he could to squelch the story. Although he was unsuccessful in preventing its publication by the *Call-Bulletin,* he was successful censoring the specific details of the attack. Despite this story in the *Call-Bulletin,* the Navy took the position that the submarine raid never occurred.

According to captured official documents detailing Japanese submarine activity along the West Coast, it was later proven that the morning of December 23, 1941 had been a busy one for the Japanese subs. A few hours earlier, Sub I-17 had fired a prematurely exploding torpedo at the Atlantic Richfield tanker, ***S.S. Larry H. Doheny,*** and had chased it to the Estero Bay Standard Oil pier. Although it escaped this time, it was later sunk in Oregon waters, with three killed and three missing in action.

An interesting footnote to the story of the ***S.S. Montebello***: After the war, the Union Oil Company sued the government for $1.6 million. Their case stated that the ship was torpedoed inside the three-mile limit and was, thus, inside the continental United States and the responsibility of the government. The case was easily thrown out when the wreckage of the ***S S. Montebello*** was located 6 miles offshore in 850 feet of water.

After the exciting lifeboat rescue, Cambrians settled down to the long, quiet war years, marked by worry about those in battle. These years were also marked by an intensified isolation. Suddenly the beloved automobile, their connection to the world, sat, unused in garages. Not only were drivers required to drive without headlights, a dangerous feat on the treacherous, curving roads in and out of Cambria, but gas and tires, difficult to get in large cities, were nearly impossible to purchase along the Central Coast. Citizens were forced to wait patiently for the good years that were ahead.

Pinedorado

In the years just after World War II, one of Cambria's many active organizations, the Lions Club, established a tradition that still delights residents and visitors alike every year, the Pinedorado, to raise funds for a much-needed community center. Given an invaluable boost by two generous women, **Lucy Fiscalini**, who donated land to serve the youth of Cambria, and **Corrine Koontz**, who loaned $6000 for a building, the Lions began planning a festival to repay this loan.

While planning this fund-raiser, the Lions volunteered their time dismantling and moving a 110′ by 37′ surplus building from Camp San Luis Obispo. They spent two weeks there before transporting the building, now in six sections, on the 30-mile, 8-hour journey to Cambria, where a two-week reconstruction project awaited.

With the move in progress, energy was focused on raising funds to repay the loan by holding a 1949 Labor Day celebration. Delays in the dismantling and transporting of the building forced postponement of this celebration until November 11, 1949. Named Pinedorado by **Bea Becker**, it was so successful that $1000 was raised. Several subsequent Labor Day Pinedorados cleared up the entire loan and, by 1953, the building, known as the Veterans' Memorial, was given to the county. This Lions Club project was such fun for the community, that Pinedorados have continued every year since. Not only have they generated a great deal of money for the community, they have also become a well-loved festivity attended by locals and visitors from all over California.

Although all are memorable, one of these early Pinedorados had a unique beginning: On the eve of the 1954 Pinedorado, Cambria experienced its first bank robbery. According to the *San Luis Obispo Tribune* of September 3, 1954:

> *Led by a nervous gunman who fumbled and dropped his pistol, two unmasked men held up the Bank of America branch at Cambria at 3 p.m. yesterday and escaped with $5600. The entire operation was performed so smoothly*

that Sheriff Murray C. Hathaway believes that the bandits had cased the bank, the community, and possible escape routes for about a month.

Branch manager C. P. Olivera, Paul Rapp, assistant cashier, and Barbara Helen Dunlap, who was the vault teller and general ledger bookkeeper, were bound with thin cord and white adhesive tape.

"Lie still if you want to stay healthy" the man holding the gun threatened.

He dropped the gun once, breaking the butt, but quickly retrieved the weapon and the broken piece.

Luckily, the robbers did not open the cash cabinet, for it contained $40,000 in cash ready for Pinedorado and the payroll for Bechtel Corporation employees who were building Morro Bay's Pacific Gas and Electric plant. In addition to being Cambria's first bank robbery, it was also the first bank robbery in more than 100 years in San Luis Obispo County. Despite extensive local and FBI searches, the robbers were never caught.

World War II had ended, automobiles were on the road again, and Cambrians were having fun with their Pinedorado. Many believed that the long-awaited years of prosperity were just around the corner. They were right, for a castle was about to bring even more changes to Cambria.

Hearst Castle

William Randolph Hearst's death in 1951 heralded huge changes for his Castle, changes that would also have a significant impact on Cambria. Built as a county home for one of the country's most powerful and wealthy men, upon his death, it was offered to California to become the "Jewel in the Crown" of California's growing State Park system, open for all to enjoy. Cambria citizens were jubilant!

Alas, there were some tense days, for the California State Legislature had to ratify this acquisition. After sailing easily through the Senate, it got stuck in the Assembly. It soon became clear that some believed that accepting Hearst Castle would be saddling California with "a white elephant of unimaginable magnitude."

To the relief of Cambrians, the acquisition was finally approved. California now had a castle, and Cambria had an amazing tourist magnet just around the corner. When this wondrous place, one of the only private country homes left intact and almost certainly the most opulent of them, was opened to the public in 1958, Cambrians saw a bright future as a prosperous tourist supply and service center. They also envisioned ever-escalating land prices and sophisticated new planned communities. At last, Cambria was on the main road to one of California's most-visited tourist destinations.

Additionally, by 1962, the road between Morro Bay and Cambria had been so significantly improved, that driving time, once 8 to 14 hours in good weather, had been reduced to 40 minutes. Many believed that Cambria was also about to become San Luis Obispo's fashionable bedroom community, opening up some exciting possibilities for growth and prosperity.

Re-designing Cambria

In 1964, while Cambrians were still celebrating their good luck, they found themselves facing yet another serious challenge. With the intention of getting tourists to Hearst Castle more quickly, a Highway 1 expressway bypass was constructed, making it all too easy for tourists bound for the Castle to miss Cambria entirely. Daunted, but not beaten, West Cambria, abutting Highway 1, was expanded to supply and serve travelers en route to the Castle. It accomplished its purpose. Unfortunately, many Highway 1 Castle-bound travelers completely missed the heart of Cambria, located several miles away.

Another challenge came with Cambria's success. As hundreds of thousands of tourists saw West Cambria, via the Castle, and growing numbers of others discovered the peaceful charm of old Cambria, many fell in love with the area and vowed to return to stay. Many did, and the escalation of land values intensified. As speculators acquired more and more land, Cambria's consistent agricultural economic base began to disappear. In these times of high hopes and high land prices, Cambria faced the decline of agriculture, its traditional economic anchor.

Suddenly, Cambria had to redefine itself. No longer able to count on its agriculture to support it during both boom and bust times, Cambrians were forced to look with a critical eye to the future of the town they loved. As the 1960s drew to a close, a few of the brave ones began to answer the question: "Would Cambria forfeit its charm and deep historical roots to become just another prosperous, crowded tourist town?" They replied with a resounding "No!"

They knew that some who had flooded California's towns after World War II wanted more than crowded suburbs full of strip malls and look-alike houses. They also wanted more than another coastal beach town full of surfers and t-shirt shops. They wanted a town with a quiet charm, old buildings that whispered of a time past, and tree-studded hills overlooking a breathtaking rock-strewn coast. They wanted Cambria!

Luckily, the Cambria they found was successful in redefining itself. Remaining a small, close-knit community, it expanded to become the perfect retreat for those seeking isolation from the hustle of much of California. It succeeded in designing the perfect place for those who demanded a unique and special town, unlike any other.

Isolation Equals Charm, 1964-Present

While Cambria does not have a movie theater, it does have a front row seat to nature's show at sunset each evening. As the time approaches, visitors and locals alike gravitate to the bluff-top walkway overlooking Moonstone Beach. And, year-round, clear or foggy, what a show it is!

Awaiting Cambria's marvelous sunsets, folks with time to spare saunter up and down downtown streets, renowned for their art galleries, specialty shops, boutiques, and antique stores. Once housing service and supply businesses, these same charming historical buildings now contain businesses committed to serve the needs of the 6500 locals and between 1.5 and 2 million visitors who enjoy Cambria every year. With neither fast food outlets, shopping malls, nor nightclubs, Cambria has re-designed itself to cater to all the needs of those who seek stunning scenery, abundant wildlife, quiet restaurants with excellent food, and a slower pace. It has done an extraordinary job of accomplishing exactly that.

This success has not been easy, and challenges still loom. Throughout much of its history, Cambria has embraced the entrepreneurial dream of a constantly growing city. It took a new breed of visionary Cambrians to cease the century-long battle against isolation and to celebrate their unique, small, and charming community. Unfortunately, just as Cambria citizens were enjoying their quiet community, so different from today's fast-changing cities, they began to face some daunting growth issues. Suddenly, many, seeking homes away from a frantic pace, discovered Cambria. While between 1990 and 2000, Cambria grew from 5382 to 5600, a slow but steady growth, a year later, the population had grown to 6690. In addition to this growth, projections forecast even more dramatic increases in the years to come.

Some of those who are flooding into the small town are World War II Baby Boomers, escaping from their jobs early to claim their corner of serenity before the flood of still other Baby Boomers seeking retirement homes. Others are young workers desiring a better place to raise their families who can, due to the wonders of technology, work and live anywhere they choose. This parade of new residents will pose a host of water and land use issues that will sorely challenge those committed to retaining the charm of this little corner of paradise.

Water: Too Much, Too Little

The history of Cambria is marked by devastating floods. Located in a long narrow valley along the Santa Rosa Creek, it has been extremely vulnerable to flooding. Often during the winter, especially the winter of 1913-14, rains continued until the soil was saturated, Santa Rosa Creek was raging, and downtown streets were underwater. Cesspools flooded and many wells were contaminated. During those times, Campbell's protected water storage cisterns, constructed in response to the Fire of 1889, played a significant role in protecting the health of Cambria citizens. Another, even worse flood swamped Cambria during the winter of 1956-57. This one was more damaging because many of the natural gullies had been filled in and buildings been built along the lowland near the estuary. During that flood, water at high tide was so deep that it poured into the windows of the businesses that had been built on the lowland.

Many Cambrians believed that their vulnerability to floods ended when Highway 1 was re-routed to bypass Cambria en route to Hearst Castle. At that time, an enormous amount of fill was used to elevate the roadbed running between the creek and stores in the lower section of the town near the ocean. They were wrong. In 1995, another flood soaked Cambria when floodwaters, reaching 9 feet, deluged West Village.

Ironically, despite the frequency of floods, when water problems are discussed in Cambria today, the discussion focuses on the scarcity of water. All realize that Cambria faces enormous water shortages as the number of homes multiply and the inevitable drought cycles continue. In response to these growth issues, the Cambria

Community Services District (CCSD) was organized in 1976 to consolidate all of Cambria's utility services. This board had some immediate success when it acquired the right to pump water from San Simeon Creek. It then began decades of study to address Cambria's looming water problems.

As the 20th century drew to a close, the CCSD was ready to begin the first phase of a $16 million reverse osmosis plant. Cambria citizens rebelled and voted out most of the board members. Instead of the large reverse osmosis plant, a smaller, far less expensive one was proposed. This plant, designed to protect Cambria from drought, but not guaranteed to accommodate the growth that many see as inevitable, leaves some of Cambria's water (and growth) issues unanswered. Hopefully, the Water Master Plan currently being developed will answer some of these questions.

Land Use Challenges

In recent years, Cambria has been the scene of extreme tension between pro- and anti-development forces. Those supporting development see growth as the road to prosperity, escalating land values, and vibrancy. Others believe adamantly that such growth will destroy Cambria's unique charm and bring the mediocrity that plagues so many other California towns. Although these two forces have battled over a number of development proposals—and development forces have often won—some recent anti-development victories, East West Ranch and the Hearst Ranch, have made headlines.

East West Ranch, between Cambria and West Cambria, was initially called Town Ranch. It was one of the pieces of property Joseph Fiscalini bought when, full of hope and energy, he was able to amass enough money to begin buying his own land. When he died and left it to his daughter, **Lucy**, this property was considered to be of little use for agricultural purposes. Eventually Lucy sold portions of the property and donated other portions, such as today's sites of the Veterans' Memorial Building, Public Library, and the relocated Santa Rosa Schoolhouse.

The remaining land, more than 400 acres, rich in ocean views and including over a mile of ocean bluff property, was the focus of a 2-decade controversy. This controversy began when Lucy's descendants, **Louis** and **Betty Fiscalini**, faced a financial crisis that forced them to sell their property. They owed over $1 million in inheritance taxes. (Between 1970 and 1990, 7 members of the large Fiscalini clan died, each death adding to a rapidly accumulating death tax debt.) In an attempt to avoid selling it to a developer, they fervently tried to convince the Coastal Conservancy to purchase the property. It was only when the Coastal Conservancy decided to purchase the Channel Islands, instead, that the Fiscalinis agreed to sell the property to a limited partnership, Rancho Pacifica.

Rancho Pacifica proposed several development plans for the property, one of which included 266 homes, an 18-hole golf course, an 18.5-acre public park on the bluff, lakes, a senior center, and 200 units of senior housing. Community opposition was so strong and water concerns so serious that approval of each of their plans was denied. By 1989, Rancho Pacifica had filed Chapter 11 bankruptcy, unable to pay their bank loan and their debt to the Fiscalinis.

In the early 1990s, four individuals, two from Southern California and two from Hong Kong, purchased the land for $2.95 million and announced they were going to establish ranches – plus a few private homes. Their plans faced another round of local opposition, conflict with the county for roads and water, and environmental outrage. Finally, by June 1999, the American Land Conservancy purchased an option to buy and protect this precious property, a purchase that was finalized in November 2000. With the consummation of this deal, an enormous chunk of old Cambria had been preserved so that one can, thankfully, still visualize Joe Fiscalini on the crest of the hill, beckoning his cows home.

Another amazing victory, for those who want Cambria to remain as it is, was announced in December 2002. It involves one of the key families in Cambria's history: the Hearsts. The property in question is the 82,000 acres of coastal and cattle land surrounding the Hearst Castle. Populated by threatened red-legged frogs, endangered steelhead trout, several unique species of oak, thousands of elephant seals, and some of the progeny of the exotic species William Randolph imported, including aoudads (wild African sheep), zebras, elk, and Asian deer, the retention of this land in its natural state is of significant importance. According to Susan Jordan, Director of the California Coastal Connection Network (*Santa Barbara News-Press*, December 9, 2002), "This particular deal is taking probably the most precious resource and open space in California that we have left."

In a recently announced agreement, the Hearsts have promised to abandon their resort development plans, including a luxury golf resort, 244 home sites, and a 650-room hotel. In exchange, they have asked for the right to build homes on 27 lots and a small inn in Old San Simeon, using old, just discovered plans by Hearst Castle architect, **Julia Morgan**. In addition, they have promised to continue working their cattle ranch, create public trails along the entire 18-mile stretch of the coast, and guarantee public access to much of the oceanfront acreage.

Preliminary negotiations, begun in 2001 with the Nature Conservancy and the Conservation Fund, broke off, but were reinitiated with the American Land Conservancy. The Conservancy is currently negotiating the amount to be paid to the Hearsts (rumored to be in excess of $100 million) for their forfeited development rights. Although the deal has not yet been finalized, many are jubilant about this incredible opportunity to preserve an important piece of history. With its completion, the Hearsts, so central to the history of Cambria, will have provided the region with an additional invaluable legacy.

Battle to Save a Landmark

One of the reasons Cambria has been successful in re-designing itself has been its preservation of a treasure trove of historical buildings throughout its downtown. A brief walking tour of Cambria's key historical structures yields an amazingly clear, though concise, glimpse of Cambria's history.

For decades, it appeared that Cambria would lose one of its most valuable historical structures. As a battle over ownership raged, Cambrians watched helplessly as the Guthrie-Bianchini House, in the heart of downtown Cambria, crumbled. Originally built before 1871, this small, roughly built shack was sold in 1873 for $425, sold again in 1882 for $500, and was purchased by **Sarah Guthrie** for $1000 in 1883. In 1914, it was sold to **Eugenio Bianchini**, a dairyman, butcher, Prohibition whiskey smuggler, and the "master of the barbecue" for many of Cambria's famous picnics.

When his wife died in 1942, the stage was set for the battle to begin. Although their son, **"Spider" Bianchini**, lived in the house until the 1970s, the lawsuit over its ownership, plus the ownership of the property remembered as the "Bucket of Blood" Saloon and 40 undeveloped acres, began in the 1950s and did not end until 1999, when the Court demanded that the house be sold. This complex case included over a dozen heirs, many of whom had left no will and some of whom lived in Italy. Considered an "international dispute" involving the Italian Consulate, the conflict over ownership dragged on and on, while the abandoned house sank further and further toward ruin.

Guthrie-Bianchini House

Finally, in April 2001, the Cambria Historical Society purchased this property, located centrally in Cambria's downtown among artists' studios and upscale restaurants, for $500,000. Fund-raising activities are underway to acquire funding to restore it and recreate its unique historical gardens. When complete, it will be a historical museum, a community center, and a public garden. Altered and enlarged frequently, it provides Cambria with an illustrated history of each of the phases of its early residential development, beginning as a simple saltbox made of locally milled wood, and becoming a complex and elaborate example of Greek Revival architecture. To be accepted by the National Register of Historic Places when it is restored, Cambria will have successfully rescued an important piece of its history.

Embracing Uniqueness

Established on an important route and seemingly destined to become a commercial center, Cambria was temporarily transformed into a mining boomtown, but soon became an isolated agricultural center. Throughout these changes, Cambrians have sought growth for their beloved town. To many, it seems that they have finally learned to embrace its isolation.

Cambria has developed into the perfect destination for travelers weary of crowds, strip malls, fast food, and traffic jams. Midway between San Francisco and Los Angeles, almost 2 million people visit it each year, either to stop briefly for refreshment before continuing to Hearst Castle, or to joyously settle into one of its many delightful inns, for peace, great beaches, wonderful restaurants, and an incredible array of art studios and galleries. Some decide to stay, as witnessed by Cambria's proliferation of successful real estate companies. Most visitors, however, simply want to enjoy a delightful respite from their 21st century challenges, coming back again and again as often as possible.

ANTIQUES
ON MAIN

Index

Sources

Although much of Cambria's history still resides in the memories of its long-time residents and resonates throughout the walls of its old buildings, many published sources were also useful. As you continue your exploration of Cambria's wonderful history, you may want to follow the trails these references provide.

And the Wind Blows Free, by Margaret Page Nemoede, September, 1988.

Chronicles of the Cambria Pioneers, by Marcus L. Waltz, 1946. Published by *The Cambrian,* Cambria, California.

Closing the Gap, Excerpts from the San Luis Obispo Morning Tribune, compiled by Wilmar Tognazzini, 1890 and 1891. Published by the *San Luis Obispo Tribune,* San Luis Obispo, California.

Hearst Castle, The Biography of a Country House, by Victoria Kastner, 2000. Published by Harry N. Abrams, New York, New York.

History of San Luis Obispo County, with Illustrations and Biographical Sketches of Its Prominent Men and Pioneers, by Myron Angel, 1883. Published by Thompson and West, Oakland, California.

History of San Luis Obispo County, State of California, Its People and Its Resources, edited by Senator Chris N. Jespersen, 1939. Published by Harold McLean Meier.

100 Years Ago, Excerpts from the *San Luis Obispo Morning Tribune,* complied by Wilmar Tognazzini, 1888 – 1902. Published by the *San Luis Obispo Tribune.*

San Luis Obispo County, by Daniel E. Krieger, 1988. Published by Windsor Publications, Northridge, California.

Stroll Down Memory Lane, Walking Tours of East Village, *Cambria Historical Society Report*, May 25, 1997.

War Comes to the Middle Kingdom, California's Central Coast Enters World War II, Volume 1, 1939-1942 by Stan Harth, Liz Krieger, Dan Krieger (editors), 1991. Published by EZ Nature Books, San Luis Obispo, California.

West Village Cambria Historical Society Walking Tour, Cambria Historical Society Report, 1988.

Where the Highway Ends, A History of Cambria, San Simeon and the Ranchos by Geneva Hamilton, 1974, 1999. Published by Central Coast Press, San Luis Obispo, California.

And, multiple articles from *The Cambrian* and the *San Luis Obispo Tribune.*

About the Author

Gayle Baker

Currently a Dean at Santa Barbara City College, I plan to retire soon to begin cruising on our sailboat, ***Anu***. My husband, Howard, Britta (our Portuguese Water Dog), and I look forward to exploring harbor towns and publishing histories of our favorites. We hope you will look for us when you visit your favorite harbor town. Joining *Catalina, Santa Barbara,* and *Cambria,* will be *Newport Beach, San Diego,* and *Point Reyes.*